VÉNUS NOIRE

RACE IN THE ATLANTIC WORLD, 1700–1900

SERIES EDITORS

Richard S. Newman, *Rochester Institute of Technology*
Patrick Rael, *Bowdoin College*
Manisha Sinha, *University of Massachusetts, Amherst*

ADVISORY BOARD

Edward Baptist, *Cornell University*
Christopher Brown, *Columbia University*
Vincent Carretta, *University of Maryland*
Laurent Dubois, *Duke University*
Erica Armstrong Dunbar, *University of Delaware
and the Library Company of Philadelphia*
Douglas Egerton, *LeMoyne College*
Leslie Harris, *Emory University*
Joanne Pope Melish, *University of Kentucky*
Sue Peabody, *Washington State University, Vancouver*
Erik Seeman, *State University of New York, Buffalo*
John Stauffer, *Harvard University*

VÉNUS NOIRE

BLACK WOMEN
AND
COLONIAL FANTASIES
IN
NINETEENTH-CENTURY FRANCE

ROBIN MITCHELL

THE UNIVERSITY OF
GEORGIA PRESS
ATHENS

© 2020 by the University of Georgia Press
Athens, Georgia 30602
www.ugapress.org
All rights reserved
Designed by Kaelin Chappell Broaddus
Set in 12/15.5 Fournier Std by Kaelin Chappell Broaddus

Most University of Georgia Press titles are
available from popular e-book vendors.

Printed digitally

Library of Congress Cataloging-in-Publication Data

Names: Mitchell, Robin, 1962– author.
Title: Vénus noire : black women and colonial fantasies in
    nineteenth-century France / Robin Mitchell.
Other titles: Black women and colonial fantasies in nineteenth-
    century France
Description: Athens, GA : The University of Georgia Press, [2020]
    | Series: Race in the Atlantic world, 1700–1900 | Includes
    bibliographical references and index.
Identifiers: LCCN 2018027405 | ISBN 9780820354323 (hard cover :
    alk. paper) | ISBN 9780820354316 (pbk. : alk. paper) | ISBN
    9780820354330 (ebook)
Subjects: LCSH: Women, Black—France—Public opinion. | Women,
    Black, in literature—France. | Women, Black, in popular
    culture—France. | Stereotypes (Social psychology)—France—
    History. | African diaspora—France. | Baartman, Sarah. |
    Duras, Claire de Durfort, duchesse de, 1777–1828. Ourika. |
    Duval, Jeanne, approximately 1820–approximately 1862—In
    literature. | Racism—France—History. | Sexism—France—
    History. | France—Race relations—History.
Classification: LCC DC34.5.A37 M58 2018 | DDC
    305.8/89604409034—dc23
LC record available at https://lccn.loc.gov/2018027405

TO CLARE.
This book literally
would not exist without you.

If I willingly tread on the unstable ground that lies between "history" and "representation," it is because I wish to blur the distinction between them.

—DORIS GARRAWAY, *The Libertine Colony*

CONTENTS

LIST OF ILLUSTRATIONS *xi*
PREFACE: Plaster Cast, an Allegory *xiii*
ACKNOWLEDGMENTS *xvii*

INTRODUCTION
Black Women in the French Imaginary *1*

CHAPTER ONE
The Tale of Three Women: The Biographies *19*

CHAPTER TWO
Entering Darkness: Colonial Anxieties and the Cultural Production of Sarah Baartmann *51*

CHAPTER THREE
Ourika Mania: Cultural Consumption of (Dis)Remembered Blackness *81*

CHAPTER FOUR
Jeanne Duval: Site of Memory *105*

CONCLUSION
Vénus Noire *135*

NOTES *141*
BIBLIOGRAPHY *161*
INDEX *177*

ILLUSTRATIONS

FIGURE 1. Eugène Delaplanche, *L'Afrique* — 2
FIGURE 2. Marie-Guillemine Benoist, *Portrait d'une négresse* — 8
FIGURE 3. Charles-Henri-Joseph Cordier, *Vénus africaine* — 20
FIGURE 4. Sophie de Tott, *Ourika* — 25
FIGURE 5. Ourika's signature, from declaration of emancipation, 1794 — 27
FIGURE 6. Ourika's signature, 1798 — 27
FIGURE 7. Anonymous, *Ourika* — 29
FIGURE 8. Broadside advertising the Hottentot Venus — 31
FIGURE 9. Sarah Baartmann's baptismal certificate — 35
FIGURE 10. Sarah Baartmann's body cast — 39
FIGURE 11. Sarah Baartmann's body cast — 52
FIGURE 12. Louis-Léopold Boilly, *Galeries du Palais-Royal* — 53
FIGURE 13. Louis François Charon and Aaron Martinet, *Les Curieux en extase; ou, Les Cordons des souliers* — 73
FIGURE 14. Aaron Martinet, *Le Prétexte* — 76
FIGURE 15. Anonymous, *Les Deux Époques* — 77
FIGURE 16. Anonymous, *Portrait d'Ourika* — 82
FIGURE 17. Erased image of Jeanne Duval — 106
FIGURE 18. Charles Baudelaire, drawing of Jeanne Duval — 113
FIGURE 19. Charles Baudelaire, drawing of Jeanne Duval — 114
FIGURE 20. Charles Baudelaire, drawing of Jeanne Duval — 115
FIGURE 21. Charles Baudelaire, drawing of Jeanne Duval — 116
FIGURE 22. Gustave Courbet, *L'Atelier du peintre* — 118
FIGURE 23. Emile Durandeau, *Les Nuits de Monsieur Baudelaire* — 119
FIGURE 24. Édouard Manet, *La Maîtresse de Baudelaire allongée* — 121
FIGURE 25. Josephine Baker — 136

PREFACE

PLASTER CAST, AN ALLEGORY

When I first arrived in Paris in 2004 to begin my research, I faced the bureaucracy of France naked in a cultural sense. French bureaucratic protocol has its special flavors: letters establishing credentials, permission for archival access, identity photos in hand, and of course, a prayer that the archivists will understand your sad French accent and lack of familiarity with the appropriate etiquette. I knew all of this when I showed up at the Musée de l'homme (*sans* appointment, *sans* letter, *sans* photos). "Could I see her?" I asked in my most proper French. "Sarah Baartmann. May I see her?" The front desk staff looked at me quizzically, as if I were an alien. Scared to death, I remained standing and quiet. Probably convinced that security would need to be engaged, they phoned upstairs to ask if someone could "do something" with me. I was then met by Philippe Mennecier, a senior curator. He was the only one available, for I had arrived at lunchtime (another major faux pas).

M. Mennecier, an extremely tall man with kind eyes behind glasses, asked what he could do for me. "Ah, Mme. Baartmann," he said softly, without a hint of condescension. "Oui," I countered. He paused for a moment, smiled, and said, "Bon. Allons-y." And with that, we went to his office, where I explained in fractured French that I had studied Baartmann for my master's thesis and was now working on her for my doctoral dissertation. I knew that her body had been repatriated to South Africa but was eager to see if anything remained from her time in the museum. He told me that many items were still there, including her body cast. Did I wish to see it?

It might be difficult for the nonhistorian to understand seeing in the flesh what you have studied for a long time (in my case, more than a decade) in pictures or books. Did I wish to see it? Yes. I don't know if I answered out loud or if I said anything else. The body cast had not been displayed for a very long time, and access to it was restricted—appropriately. I had assumed that the cast had been repatriated along with most of the museum's other Baartmann-related holdings in 2001, but the South African government had not wanted everything. The cast was brought out in an immense crate. As I waited and watched the screws holding the cover in place being removed with a power drill, my sense of anticipation began to rise. I started pacing. I am a historian, I told myself; this reaction is unprofessional. As the unpacking continued, the feelings worsened. I was having trouble breathing. I began peering at the skeletons lined up along one wall, wondering who these people were. My hands were shaking. The last screw was removed. I held my breath. They pulled. Nothing happened. "Merde," the technician complained. Ah, they had missed one screw.

The technician left me alone with M. Mennecier and the crate. M. Mennecier removed the cover, and I burst into tears. Horrified by my own reaction, I begged M. Mennecier's pardon. "Non, pas du tout. C'est normal." He then asked in English if I would like a moment alone with her. I nodded, and he departed. I sat in the chair next to her and wept. I do not know for how long. Then I placed my hand in her tiny plaster hand and promised her, "I'll try not to screw this up." I left the room. After that, Philippe, as he let me call him, and I had many "dates" with Mme. Baartmann. I remain grateful to him for the kindness and subsequent friendship he showed a clueless graduate student that day. Meeting Sarah Baartmann remains a difficult and profound memory for me. I tell it here because history matters. The lives of the long-dead people we write about still matter, and the way we tell these stories undeniably matters. To pretend that I am not implicated in the stories contained in this book would be a lie. In fact, one of the reasons Baartmann first caught my attention is because of the uncanny similarities between her body and mine. Discovering the women I write about in this book was a progressive revelation. They changed everything for me. What I thought I knew about France I did not know.

This responsibility does not mean I cannot tell the stories about these women and their lives—I can. As a historian, I can read the documents and interpret the silences. As an African American woman involved in cultural work about black women's bodies, the personal *is* political. Moreover, as I convey here, the women discussed in this book were not saints: they were human beings who often endured terrible suffering and degradation. And they sometimes reacted to their treatment with extreme anger and violence. I hope that each of these women had periods of laughter and joy as well.

ACKNOWLEDGMENTS

This project took a very long time to come to fruition, and it took a village to get to this moment. Mentors, teachers, colleagues, family, and friends made this work possible. My dissertation adviser at the University of California, Berkeley, Tyler Stovall, first met me as an undergraduate and guided me through graduate school. The journey hasn't always been pretty, but I have been able to complete it because of your faith in me. I thank Carla Hesse for support that continued long after I graduated. You kept every promise. Susanna Barrows, I miss you every single day. I thank Walter Biggins, Bénédicte Dazy, Ellen Goldlust, Thomas Roche, and the rest of the staff at the University of Georgia Press, who helped an amateur become a writer, and the Race in the Atlantic World series editors, who saw promise in this work in its first iterations. The two anonymous readers provided thoughtful suggestions for revising the manuscript that improved it immeasurably. Sue Peabody has quietly and steadfastly shepherded so many of us to this moment. I lack the words. My research assistants—Alexandra Chapman, Matthew Gin, Kaleb Knoblauch, Johanna Montlouis-Gabriel, Caren Scott, and Clare Stuber—helped with translations, tracked down documents, brought sustenance, and kept me sane.

I am grateful to the colleagues who reviewed chapters, offered advice and encouragement, led me to sources, and without question made this book stronger: Mary Alice and Philip Boucher, Pierre

Boulle, Claire Garcia, Jennifer Heuer, Amy Aisen Kallander, Jennifer Palmer, Alison Locke Perchuk, Mark Sawchuk, Rebecca Hartkopf Schloss, and Lorelle Semley. I am grateful to Philippe Mennecier at the Musée de l'homme (and more recently of the Jardin des plantes) for his gracious assistance and kind friendship and for making me believe that "tout est possible." This project has benefited from almost twenty years of archival research, and I'm deeply grateful for the assistance of the Archives départementales Paris; the Archives départementales de Loire-Atlantique, Nantes; the Archives Municipales de Bordeaux; the Archives de Nantes; the Archives Nationales, Paris; the Archives nationales d'outre-mer, Aix-en-Provence; the Bibliothèque nationale de France, Paris; the Bibliothèque Sainte-Geneviève, Paris; the British Library, London; the Collection Achac Research Group, Paris; the Collection Grob/Kharbine-Tapabor, Paris; the Hulton Archive; the Jardin des plantes, Paris; the Musée de l'homme, Paris; and the National Archives, London. Thank you also to Eric Saugera for teaching me so much about the history of slavery in Bordeaux and Nantes.

While at DePaul University, I benefited from research funds for conferences and travel, for which I remain grateful. Portions of chapters 1 and 3 were originally published elsewhere and are reprinted by permission of the publisher: "Shaking the Racial and Gender Foundations of France: The Influences of 'Sarah Baartmann' in the Production of Frenchness," in *Black French Women and the Struggle for Equality, 1848–2015* (Lincoln: University of Nebraska Press, 2018); "Another Means of Understanding the Gaze: Sarah Bartmann and the Development of Nineteenth-Century French National Identity," in *They Called Her Hottentot: The Art, Science, and Fiction of Sarah Baartman*, ed. Deborah Willis and Carla Williams (Philadelphia: Temple University Press, 2010), 32–46. In addition, portions of chapter 2 were originally published in "'Ourika Mania': Interrogating Race, Class, Space, and Place in Early 19th-Century France," *African and Black Diaspora: An International Journal* 10, no. 2 (2017): 85–95, and are reprinted by permission of the publisher. A number of conferences helped me present, refine, and revise this work. Any errors remain my own.

Since 2016, the History Department at California State University, Channel Islands, has been my home. Department heads Jim Meriwether and Frank Barajas have made me feel I have a place here. I am also lucky to work with good colleagues and a wonderful library staff. The Office of Research and Sponsored Programs and the Provost's Office provided much-needed funding for illustrations. Thank you.

Among the friends and colleagues to whom I owe thanks are Noliwe Alexander, Robin Bates, Dana Baker, Mori Benjamin, Aiden Bettine, Constance Bryan, Corey Capers, Kristina Del Pino, Naomi Dushay, Julie Moody Freeman, Molly Giblins, Bert Gordon, Aimee Hammond, Mette Harder, Colleen Harris, Sandra Harvey, Elizabeth Hollon, Sarah Horowitz, Elizabeth Kelly, Daniel Klein, Larry Lytle, Lowry Martin, Brinda Mehta, Matthew Mendez, Sunny McFadden, Rob Robbins, Rosetta Saunders, Bryan Sykes, Kat St. Thomas, Luke Teausaw, Monique Wells, Sheridan Wiggington, and Sarah Zimmerman. I am more grateful to my Black Women's Experiences classes at DePaul University than words can express. Thank you all from the bottom of my heart.

I also could not have completed this project without the support—moral and otherwise—of my family. My parents, Edward and Loretta Mitchell, the two constants in a sea of change (I miss you so much, Mom), and my brother, Guy Mitchell, saw this book as a foregone conclusion even when it existed only in my mind. David Carr still makes me laugh, is a genius, and quite simply saved my life. Clare Stuber went from student to legit family in minutes. And Mitchell Dushay: it was serendipitous that I found you. I am grateful, and I love you.

VÉNUS NOIRE

INTRODUCTION

BLACK WOMEN IN THE FRENCH IMAGINARY

> If skin is the only difference then the Negro might be considered a black European. The Negro is, however, so noticeably different from the European that one must look beyond skin color.
> —SAMUEL THOMAS VON SOEMMERRING as quoted in Londa Schiebinger, "Skeletons in the Closet"

From the seventeenth century into the nineteenth, all the major European powers (Portugal, Spain, England, France, Scotland, Denmark, Sweden, and the Netherlands) participated enthusiastically in the slave trade. However, even though the colonies supported lavish lifestyles in Europe, Europeans went to considerable lengths to disguise the extent to which buying and selling human beings was a lucrative enterprise. As late as 1830, fifteen years after France formally abolished the slave trade, it engaged more of the country's ships than did legitimate commerce.[1] Despite efforts to conceal the French involvement, the country remained directly and actively involved in—and benefited from—the buying and selling of people of African descent. While European cities such as Paris, London, and Madrid were hailed as bastions of *cosmopolitanism* (they were, in a technical sense) and achieved that cosmopoli-

FIGURE 1.

Eugène Delaplanche (1836–91), *L'Afrique*, 1878.
L'Afrique is one of six allegorical statues representing the six continents created for the Exposition Universelle (World's Fair) in 1878 that now line the esplanade in the courtyard of the Musée d'Orsay, Paris. All six of the statues had been improperly cared for in Nantes for almost fifty years before being purchased and returned to Paris in 2013.

tan status partly via riches reaped from their slave colonies, they were, in fact, also *imperial* cities. This distinction is important, since notions of cosmopolitanism can conceal a multitude of sins that cannot be hidden behind the *imperial* or *colonial* label. In short, presenting oneself as merely cosmopolitan had long-standing cultural repercussions; as a consequence of the ongoing attempts to prevent the practice of slavery from touching (and thereby tarnishing) France proper, the French could minimize their active participation in the slave trade.

In the eighteenth century, metropolitan France had a tiny nonwhite population—about three thousand people out of a population of more than twenty-five million as of 1777.[2] However, the French colonies—particularly Martinique, Saint-Domingue, and other Caribbean possessions that had extensive sugar and coffee plantations—had substantial numbers of people of color. Despite this geographical distance from the metropole, images of and discussions about people of color, especially women, frequently appeared in a variety of French cultural sectors and social milieus. Paradoxically, although mainland France had minimal numbers of black women, their bodies attracted a disproportionate amount of attention. However, they were more than mere curiosities or aesthetic fodder, and as this book demonstrates, the literary and visual depictions of black women gave rise to cultural discourses about Frenchness that shaped the country's postrevolutionary national identity. Black women helped France's white men and women fantasize about their black colonies and often served as substitutes for making sense of white bodies "behaving badly."

Highly negative discourses regarding black slaves appeared in some of the earliest seventeenth-century French missionary accounts.[3] In the late seventeenth and early eighteenth centuries, a second wave of anxiety emerged around racial mixing in the colonies. In metropolitan France, a flurry of legislation attempted to calm fears of racial inundation and contamination.[4] Existing representations of black women in the colonies were subsequently appropriated, deployed, recycled, and repurposed, circulating more widely in the metropole. As Sue Peabody has shown, blacks were often depicted as symbols for political and social positioning for white Frenchmen.[5] Though the rhetoric stressed that France had no slaves, the country's livelihood largely depended on slavery in the colonies as well as at home. This contradiction complicated the functionality of these opposing rhetorical strategies yet made these interactions more meaningful. This awareness creates a new space for understanding how different locations in Europe constructed and reconstructed themselves and their colonial Others and relocates our understanding of geopolitical thinking to a much earlier period in French history. This book examines how science and popular culture simultaneously informed and regulated social behavior. It also considers the extent to which existing boundaries of that time period separated scientific discourse from popular entertainment, thereby demonstrating the fallacy of such constraints. Portrayals of the black female body allowed white Frenchwomen to discuss issues of race and gender, while white Frenchmen could use the black female body to discuss white women, black women, *and* black men, thus layering many social and political tensions onto one body.

HAITI AND THE FRENCH REVOLUTION

Depictions of black people in eighteenth- and nineteenth-century French discourse were not static but changed in response to events, particularly the French and Haitian Revolutions. The French Revolution of 1789 created tremendous upheaval for notions of citizenship and nationhood in France, raising questions about such topics as who was now eligible to vote and the roles that Jews, Arabs, and others would play in the new nation.[6] In addition, the revolution had less-well-known consequences for French understandings of race and gender that were epitomized in the Haitian Revolution of 1791–1804. Saint-Domingue had been the crown jewel of France's first colonial empire; the uprising there took the lives of thirty thousand white

Frenchmen and other Europeans, and permanently drove the French completely from the island of Hispaniola. No modern European power had ever suffered a defeat of such magnitude at the hands of blacks, and Haiti remains the only nation in the world founded on the basis of a slave rebellion.

For more than two centuries, the French tended to downplay the significance of the revolution in Saint-Domingue, with many eighteenth-century white Frenchmen and -women dismissively referring to it as the "troubles."[7] In fact, Jeremy Popkin notes that the French government went to great lengths to suppress news of the uprising in Saint-Domingue, censoring publications to prevent them from "evoking the memory of the humiliating French defeat in Saint-Domingue."[8] Similarly, the continued French use of the term *Saint-Domingue* long after the independent nation adopted the name *Haiti*, as Alyssa Sepinwall argues, indicates an official reluctance to acknowledge that the colony no longer belonged to France.[9] As William Cohen concludes, the French government clung to the belief that either by concession or by force, Saint-Domingue could be recaptured and the institution of slavery reimposed.[10] For Sepinwall, the surprising lack of historical attention paid to Haiti even in modern-day France can be ascribed in part to the fact that "race is anathema in contemporary French discourse."[11]

Yet any sustained analysis of the Haitian Revolution reveals that this event was cataclysmic, sending shock waves throughout the Atlantic world. Even before the 1789 revolution, France had been struggling with a series of imperial losses that began in Canada and India in the 1760s. And as the nation was struggling with the thorny issues of citizenship and national identity brought on by the revolution, it had to grapple not only with the loss of its most important colony but also with the 1803 sale of Louisiana to the United States. Even standard terms used to describe French constitutional history since 1799 such as the *Empire* and the *Second Empire* elide the true imperial history and legacy of defeat. The loss of Haiti and the collapse of Napoleon's empire threatened France's self-perception as an imperial power (with its connotations of racial superiority) and its image of its masculine prowess.

As Krishan Kumar writes, "Nations are formed of national memories, of the stories of great men and great deeds. . . . But it is not just triumphs and glory but also, and perhaps more so, defeats and trials that make the nation."[12] Haiti was a thrashing and a trial that would not be easily overcome. The geopolitical and social consequences were immediate: between six thousand and ten thousand white Creoles fled to metropolitan France following the collapse of French rule in Saint-Domingue.[13] Most of the refugees landed in Paris, where they were, for all practical purposes, foreign. They formed part of an enormous migration both into and out of France over the revolutionary and Napoleonic years. After 1789, France experienced nearly two decades of constant population movements, including returning soldiers from the Napoleonic Wars, diehard ultraroyalist émigrés, and military and colonial refugees from Haiti, all of whom brought new customs, values, and cultural identities with them. In many cases, assimilating or reassimilating in the midst of continuous political upheavals was neither a simple nor a happy experience.

The vast majority of the migrants from Saint-Domingue were white settlers, with only about eight hundred blacks fleeing the colony.[14] Yet when Saint-Domingue violently and permanently unyoked itself from France, the cultural reverberations both fueled and haunted the ongoing discursive construction of race and gender. In particular, the representations of black women (who probably represented a small minority among the influx) illuminate these tensions. As art historian James Smalls maintains, defining and empowering the colonial (and postcolonial) self was of paramount importance to white Frenchmen and -women.[15] This volume explores the psychological ramifications of this defeat for the nation, revealing the extent to which France was dealing with threats to white racial homogeneity much earlier than has previously been realized.[16] Writers, artists, politicians, and French laypeople situated and attempted to mitigate these traumas through the black female body, seeking ways to redefine Frenchness and bury the anxieties raised by the defeat in Haiti. The book investigates the eroticization of the black female body and the simultaneous need to disavow that body. The trauma of losing Saint-Domingue was displaced onto a body and in a manner that appeared to simplify a far more complex range of experiences and identities.

CULTURAL REPRESENTATIONS AND NATIONAL IDENTITY

Hanging in the Musée du Louvre is Marie-Guillemine Benoist's painting *Portrait d'une négresse* (fig. 2).[17] Painted in 1800, the unnamed black woman faces her audience with her breast exposed in an explicitly sexualized way.[18] Her arm hugs her dress in a gesture that seems intended to keep her other breast from also being revealed. She is surrounded by the accoutrements of luxury—the sumptuous shawl and the beautiful chair—but the plainness of the woman's white dress, her lack of identification (her name was in fact Madeleine), and most important her skin color show that she is merely an ornament of her mistress or master's wealth. Her direct and somewhat intimate stare at the viewer is enigmatic, and her blue shawl, red sash, and white dress evoke the colors of revolution, a trope that hardly applies in her case, however.[19] Finally, her head covering constitutes a colonial marker of her blackness and confirms her subjugated status. Her passivity (or resignation) invites a sustained and sexualized gaze. She is eroticized and touchable, as much a product for consumption as the accessories surrounding her. Observers have suggested that this image is reminiscent of Jacques-Louis David's portrait of Mme. Récamier both in pose and artistic style and that given the date when *Portrait d'une négresse* was painted, the image could be interpreted as a celebration of French abolitionism.[20] David's portrayal of her as fully clothed, as well as his use of her given name, shows a greater respect for his subject. And while the woman in *Por-*

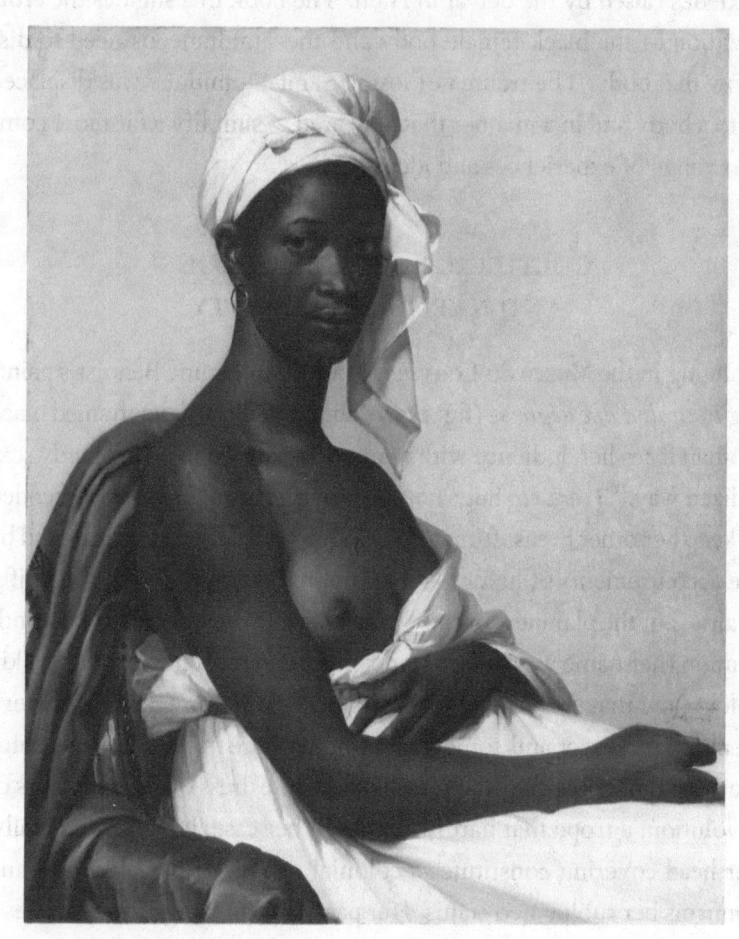

FIGURE 2.

Marie-Guillemine Benoist (1768–1826), *Portrait d'une femme noire* (also known as *Portrait d'une négresse*), 1800. Benoist was one of the few female students of the painter Jacques-Louis David. Musée du Louvre, Paris.

trait d'une négresse gazes at the viewer, she lacks the look of agency. Did Benoist know her name? If the woman was truly a subject of worth, why not acknowledge that more fully by naming her? British art historians Hugh Honour and John Fleming suggest that Benoist may have used the painting to advocate for women's emancipation. If so, it seems clear that this emancipation did not extend to black women.[21]

Nineteenth-century French cultural representations of black women reflect earlier historical events going back to the establishment of France's Caribbean colonies in the seventeenth and eighteenth centuries. The social and economic conditions of slavery in Martinique and elsewhere generated pervasive tropes about black women that made their way to metropolitan France, where they provided a surprisingly attractive canvas that the citizens of a fragmented, traumatized, and dislocated country used to digest the ramifications of their losses. Gustave d'Eichthal, the secretary of the Société ethnologique, wrote in his 1839 *Lettres sur la race noire et la race blanche* that blacks were a "female race." "Just like the woman," he pontificated, "the black is deprived of political and scientific intelligence. . . . Like the woman he also passionately likes jewelry, dance, and singing."[22] Eichthal's assignment of a discursive gender to an entire race of people helps to illustrate how the failure in Haiti, taken as a defeat at the hands of black men, facilitated a reordering of French national identity via the black female body, which was represented as savage, hypersexual, and above all an existential threat to the purity of the French nation. Blacks could not and should not be a part of the French body politic. Eichthal reinforces the assumption that blacks were not included in the definition of Frenchness.

Representations of black bodies both in France and in the colonies show that race encouraged the development of different notions of French citizenship and subjectivity. Every regime—the Republic, the Empire, the Restoration—attempted to redefine for itself what it meant to be French, with constant debates over the meaning of liberty and equality.[23] With slavery temporarily reinstated in 1802, the distinction between free whites and enslaved blacks and the relationship between male and female bodies afforded a safer way to talk about larger issues of freedom. Paul Gilroy proposes the term *crypto-nationalism* to characterize how nationalist writers "are often disinclined to consider the cross catalytic or transverse dynamics of racial politics as a significant element in the formation and reproduction of . . . national identities."[24] This oversight is particularly curious given the collective hand-wringing and self-examination that normally follow a loss of such magnitude (Haiti), especially since the political, cultural, and military loss came at the hands of what were considered racial inferiors.[25]

For many historians, the revolutionary era forms an almost impenetrable barrier, with scholarship falling squarely on either side of the 1789 divide or narrowly within the immediate years of the revolution. Yet paying attention to colonial slavery and plantation society reveals a number of interesting continuities in the cultural production of race and gendered discourse that stretched throughout the entire Bourbon, revolutionary, and imperial eras.

As the evolving conversation about national identity suggests, ideas of Frenchness shifted from monarchy to republic to empire. Under the Bourbons, the royal family was emblematic of the nation in both image and allegory. In this "family romance," as historian Lynn Hunt calls it, "the ideology of absolutism explicitly tied royal government to the patriarchal family, and the use of the term *fraternity* during the French Revolution implied a break with this prior model."[26] Killing the king redefined Frenchness away from royal bodies and instead rooted it in brotherhood. In conjunction with concurrent social and political changes, elites used discourses on national identity to better establish and maintain social control. Under the tension and uncertainty of the revolution and the Napoleonic Code, "active" citizenship was recognized only for adult men. Women of all colors and all colonial men, regardless of race (with the exception of a brief liberal moment in 1848–52), were subordinated to male heads of household as passive citizens. According to historian Carla Hesse, women were involved in the revolution and subsequently sent back home, highlighting the importance of gender-related tensions within white French society as well.[27]

Black women, seen as Other by the new republican definition of *citoyenneté*, are a particularly rich focal point to study in exploring how France grappled with both race and gender. Yet no one has yet tackled the historical presence of and discursive focus on black women in the metropole. This book closely explores the stories of three women who achieved contemporary fame, meaning that a relative wealth of information is available about them. Each has been amply studied individually. However, this volume breaks new ground by studying them in conversation with one another, enabling scholars of France not only to reckon with the long-standing importance of black women as historical subjects but also to see how the use and production of their bodies reinforced strategies of whiteness, blackness, and Frenchness. Bringing together these women's stories provides additional information regarding the conflicts between French identity and national belonging within particular roles.[28]

The discursive presence of black women in nineteenth-century France—how they were seen, perceived, produced, and represented—suggests that French elites were deeply unsettled by the Haitian Revolution and that this disturbance contributed to an unclaimed and ignored racialized national identity. The legacy of this blind spot continues to trouble French national identity in the postcolonial present and therefore remains relevant and vital to understanding France today.

Although some scholars have studied black female representations in France, particularly in literature and art, less attention has been paid to analyzing these representations within a larger historical framework. This project brings together the social history of black women in France and cultural studies—including art history, political theory, women's and gender studies, and critical race theory.[29] Historical studies of the presence of blacks in the colonies and in France have lacked a sustained focus on black women.[30] Some scholars of literature, critical theory, gender, and art history have studied images of blacks in France and the meaning of such depictions.³¹ But tensions exist between these types of scholarship: history seeks to recover an accurate and changing past, while theories of representation look for the ways that enduring power relations, especially those built on binaries, operate as abstractions. Scholarship that seeks to incorporate both types of analytical models can be challenging: one tries to access a stable "truth" through documents, while the other insists that all documents, texts, images, or representations are distorted by powerful discourses of the dominant culture.³²

This book incorporates several distinct theoretical discussions in the fields of modern French history, ethnic studies, and race and gender studies, contributing to our understanding of the historical production of French nationalism and of gender and racial identities from the ancien régime through the first half of the nineteenth century. In addition, the volume transcends conventional periodization to look at continuities and disjunctions between prerevolutionary France and the modern era.

Marisa Fuentes writes about the often heartbreaking "constructions of enslaved women in the archival records": "enslaved women appear as historical subjects through the form and content of archival documents in the manner in which they lived: spectacularly violated, objectified, disposable, hypersexualized, and silenced. The violence is transferred from the enslaved bodies to the documents that count, condemn, assess, and evoke them, and we receive them in this condition."³³ The prevailing narrative of these representations, which transcends the vastly different political and cultural structures of multiple French regimes, established and reinforced the inability of these women to be French, regardless of their individual stories or backgrounds. Yet the representations of these women also reveal fissures in the definition of what it meant to be French, challenging existing gender and racial boundaries within white society. Too often, blackness in the French imagination (as elsewhere, though perhaps less uniformly) is often unthinkingly equated with enslavement. Scholars must remain conscious of the distinction.

How were representations of difference among black female bodies used to make sense of the loss of French colonies and to prove the importance of future imperial domination? Like blackness, Frenchness was not statically defined. That the meaning of both terms changed over time allows us to ask important questions about these constructions: How were the anxieties over shifting definitions and productions of Frenchness projected onto black bodies and specifically black female bodies? French social, cultural, and political upheavals in this transitional era hindered the crystallization of a single, concrete national identity. This book explores how—in the midst of national shock brought on by the French and Haitian Revolutions—black women came to occupy particular discursive visibility despite the fact that their actual numbers in France were very small.

Edward Said's classic study, *Orientalism*, calls attention to the importance of cultural production, reminding us that "a very large mass of writers, among whom are poets, novelists, philosophers, political theorists, economists, and imperial administrators, have accepted the basic distinction between East and West as the starting point for elaborate theories, epics, novels, social descriptions, and political accounts concerning the Orient, its people, customs, 'mind,' destiny, and so on."[34] Though focused mainly on the "Middle East," Said's insights highlight the idea that the white French writers, painters, lawyers, and so on who produced the dominant texts also played the primary role in crafting messages about black women and about Frenchness. These discussions were always in dialogue with the audiences and critics who consumed these works. In a similar vein, Robert Darnton's essay about cultural production in the information era argues that popular culture did not emanate from elites down to the lower classes or pass along single channels but rather circulated simultaneously up and down, back and forth.[35]

In keeping with this idea, this book juxtaposes a vast array of sources to contextualize the social and political environments in which images of black women circulated. These sources include artworks (paintings, prints, and sculptures), legal cases, rulings, legislation, parliamentary debates, literary works (plays, poems, memoirs, and letters), fashion (not just items of clothing but also the historical meaning they conveyed to both black and white Frenchmen and -women), and pamphlets, advertisements, and newspapers. In addition to weaving together these various genres, I incorporate scholarship from a host of disciplines, particularly feminist studies as well as cultural and social history, thereby providing a broad perspective on colonialism, race, and gender and thus a more comprehensive investigation of the historical moments in which these women lived.[36]

THE BLACK WOMEN OF ART AND FICTION

Chapter 1 introduces the three women at the heart of this study, Ourika, Sarah Baartmann, and Jeanne Duval.[37] These basic biographical sketches show not only the contours of their lives but also the challenges of reconstructing them from the scant surviving archival evidence. The next three chapters focus in turn on the literary and visual depictions of each of these women. Although the historical Ourika (ca. 1771–99) lived well before Baartmann arrived in France in 1814, "Ourika Mania" did not begin until 1823–24, when Claire de Duras published her novel *Ourika*. Consequently, chapter 2 addresses the multiple invocations of Baartmann during her lifetime, while my examination of Duras's work is reserved for chapter 3. Finally, chapter 4 centers on the life of Jeanne Duval, a working woman who was depicted using a wide range of racialized tropes, largely through the work of her common-law husband, the poet Charles Baudelaire.

Between 1786 and 1870, these three women of color altered the French social landscape in a way that could not have happened in the colonies. Because these women were real people as well as archetypes, early colonial tropes of savagery and otherworldliness worked differently when the women moved to France. Their physical existence on French soil belied the considerable cultural work of white Frenchmen and -women that strove to make them appear ahistorical. Their presence in the metropole led to cultural clashes that demanded redefinitions of Frenchness.

As chapter 2 shows, Baartmann, popularly known as the Hottentot Venus, represented the distorted memories of Haiti in the French imagination. Her display, treatment, and representation embodied the residual anger and anxieties the French harbored after losing their most important colony. Questioning the French preoccupation with the cultural need to understand the black female body demonstrates why this interest aided in understanding the white female body. Thus, the racialized as well as sexualized construction of Baartmann, despite being hidden in scientific and cultural packaging, is critical to understanding her importance at this specific historical juncture.

Chapter 3 looks at how white Frenchmen and -women appropriated black female identity through the representations of Ourika, a young Senegalese girl purchased as a house pet for the Maréchal Prince de Beauvau in 1788. More than twenty years after her death in 1799, she became the subject of numerous plays, poems, and discussions, inspiring clothing, jewelry, fashion, colors, and hairstyles. These fads allowed middle- and upper-class white Frenchwomen to wear blackness without fully transgressing French racial and gender norms. At the same time, the white Frenchmen who were writing about Ourika exposed and perpetuated stereotypes of the hypersexual black woman and emphasized the impossibility and unsuitability of her marrying a white man of her own class, thereby reinforcing her inability to sustain the breeding she had acquired in aristocratic French society. These phenomena highlight the interconnectedness of gender and race issues, especially as white women attempted to exercise some agency over their own changed circumstances and white men attempted to control both black and white women and the definition of Frenchness.

Chapter 4 looks at how these themes played out during the July Monarchy (1830–48) and into the Second Empire (1852–70) using an examination of Duval, Baudelaire's longtime lover. Baudelaire's contemporaries and subsequent biographers have demonized Duval, in part to elevate Baudelaire. The level of vitriol toward Duval, however, reveals something deeper. The chapter analyzes Duval's life as a part-time actress, prostitute, and wife within the historical context of the end of the French slave empire. The erasure of Duval's humanity becomes a metaphor for the historic need to rid France yet again of actual black bodies even as images and discourses about these bodies proliferated.

The French defined themselves in opposition to the representations of these specific historical black women. This ongoing compulsion has continued well into the current century, with black women (from anywhere) such as Josephine Baker both acting as an exotic Other and highlighting the foreignness of any black body within the French body politic.

These real historical women existed independently of their representations. They lived in France, they walked along the cobblestones, they may have had favorite pâtisseries, they spoke to people, and people spoke back to them. But the people who had power saw these women merely as objects, and that is how they survive today. There are no extant documents that allow them to speak, to tell their own stories. They continue to exist only as foils for all kinds of French imaginations, as symbols or tools, in representations of them produced for the most part by white men and women within a limited set of tropes or stereotypes. Ourika was long dead by the time images and stories of her began to circulate widely. Only one word spoken by Baartmann has been recorded: she said "No" when naturalist Georges Cuvier sought to look under her apron. Only Duval had the opportunity to push back against the stereotypes, most likely because she outlived the man who was supposed to control her representation. Although her defiance was minimal, it provoked a vicious response from Baudelaire's contemporaries, who tried to eradicate her. Nevertheless, she finally defeated the racial and gendered ventriloquism that began with Baartmann and was perfected with Ourika.

Even today, many French leaders seem eager to separate their country's history from slavery and the slave trade, imperial endeavors that contributed greatly to its economic survival and prestige. But such legacies can be fully understood only in relation to one another. This work also touches on the emergence of celebrity and consumer culture, which are generally seen as late nineteenth-century phenomena. In addition, this book fills a gap in women's histories in France, particularly by illuminating how even a small number of black women could so affect and restructure French society. Finally, this project contributes to the growing scholarship of the African diaspora in France in the nineteenth century.

This is not simply a tale of looking at black women: it is a cultural history of white Frenchmen and -women looking at black women. Black women mattered in France, as is evidenced by the tremendous amount of time and effort white Frenchmen and -women devoted to trying to convince themselves and others that black women lacked importance. This is not the story most people envision when thinking about the century following the French Revolution. These women were not supposed be there. Yet they were.

CHAPTER ONE

THE TALE OF THREE WOMEN

THE BIOGRAPHIES

A light here requires a shadow there.
—VIRGINIA WOOLF, *To the Lighthouse*

Charles-Henri-Joseph Cordier's striking 1851 bronze bust, *Vénus africaine* (fig. 3), exemplifies the visibility of black women in nineteenth-century French art. According to the Walters Art Museum in Baltimore, a young African woman served as the model for this "highly popular" sculpture, which powerfully expresses "nobility" and "human pride and dignity in the face of grave injustice." Among those who acquired casts of the sculpture were the Museum of Natural History in Paris and Queen Victoria.[1] Despite the popularity of this and other works depicting African women around the time that slavery ended in France, no one appears to have recorded the name of the "young African woman."[2] In fact, she was a formerly enslaved black woman living in France. Cordier, an abolitionist, claimed to believe in the beauty of peoples of other races, but by calling this sculpture *Vénus africaine*, he indicated that he saw no need to link it with an actual person, even though doing so might have resonated with the viewer.[3]

FIGURE 3.

Charles-Henri-Joseph Cordier (1827–1905), *Vénus africaine*, 1851.
Casts of the sculpture were done in 1851 and subsequently acquired by
both the Museum of Natural History in Paris and Queen Victoria.
Walters Art Museum, Baltimore.

More is known about the three women on whom this book focuses. Although they were separated chronologically, they were and remain connected in other ways. Ourika, Sarah Baartmann, and Jeanne Duval are essential characters in the annals of black women in France, with their shifting narratives and cultural breadth. Though real women, they are also icons: as Sander Gilman writes,

> Rather than presenting the world, icons represent it. . . . [T]he ideologically charged iconographic nature of the representation dominates. And it dominates in a very specific manner, for the representation of individuals implies the creation of some greater class or classes to which the individual is seen to belong. These classes in turn are characterized by the use of a model which synthesizes our perception of the uniformity of the groups into a convincingly homogeneous image.[4]

Although these women were iconic, they were also actual human beings, and the details of their lives are the necessary starting point for this study, providing a grounding for the chapters that follow, which examine the representations of these women and their importance to white Frenchmen and -women. This chapter explores what is known about them—often as a consequence of accounts by their own contemporaries. Introducing these women and their biographies centers their most authentic selves, establishing and emphasizing the importance of their lived realities based on the limited information available about them. Although details about their lives remain exasperatingly sparse, these women are united by the fact that, regardless of their time on French soil, they never achieved the elusive Frenchness that this book investigates.

CHARLOTTE CATHERINE BENEZET OURIKA

Documentation about the real Ourika, the young girl who inspired the protagonist of Claire de Duras's eponymous novel, remains scant, but scholars have begun to fill in some details regarding her life. Literary scholar Roger Little believes that Ourika was from Fouta-Djallon, in what is now southeastern Senegal, and that she was likely of Peul origin.[5] In early 1786, the governor of Senegal, Stanislas Jean, the Chevalier du Boufflers, purchased a two- or three-year-old Senegalese girl for the Duchesse d'Orleans.[6] This little girl, Zoé, is often confused with Ourika but was raised as a servant in the home of another aristocratic family. Boufflers described the girl as follows: "She is pretty, not like the day, but like the night.... Her eyes are like little stars.... She does not speak yet, but she understands what we say to her in Wolof." He felt "moved to tears thinking that this poor child was sold to me like a lamb," and he had become so fond of her that he feared that he would have difficulty separating from her. He also told his future wife, Delphine de Sabran, "If you see her at the Palais-Royal, don't forget to speak to her in her language and to kiss her while thinking that I have kissed her also, and that her face is the meeting point of our lips."[7] Despite his evident affection for the girl, he positions her solely as a conduit between himself and Delphine. Moreover, by using passive voice after claiming his purchase ("was sold to me"), he obscures his active role.

The following July, Boufflers wrote again to Sabran to detail some additional exotic treasures that he had acquired: "a parakeet for the queen, a horse for the maréchale de Castries, a little captive for M. de Beauvau, a sultan hen for the duke of Laon, an ostrich for M. de Nivernais and a husband for you."[8] The "little captive" was Ourika. Consciously or unconsciously, the chevalier classed Ourika alongside the other animals he brought from Senegal to be distributed as presents.[9] Boufflers apparently was well known for gifting black children to his friends and family. Sabran wrote to him that one such young boy "delighted" Elzéar and Delphine (her children). "[Y]our little savage, whom my children call Friday ... is our only source of pleasure and entertainment."[10] This "little savage" is made another consumable in the form of a toy for children to play with and then discard at their leisure.

Eighteenth-century French nobility delighted in keeping black children as the equivalent of house pets, and according to historian Shelby McCloy, "little Negro boys were often presented as gifts to persons of prominence in France by officials and planters abroad."[11] They wore elaborate costumes and accessories that had specific social functions. Historian Kate Lowe writes that in Renaissance images, "Africans (even though usually slaves and servants) are often depicted wearing beautiful and expensive jewellery.... One reason for the preponderance of other bejeweled Africans is that a large proportion of black African images come from courtly settings, where the Africans would have been clothed and adorned to show off the status of their masters."[12] Elaborately dressed, the slaves served as jesters, miniature companions, servants, and fodder for aristocratic amusements: "In France, it was the day of the exotic. Dress, furniture, decorations, foods and drinks, books, and plays smacked of the faraway—of the orient and America—and a sure way to prestige was to have a black in livery to open the door for madame's friends and to drive her carriage."[13] In 1787, Boufflers sent at least one more Senegalese child back to France, a five- or six-year-old boy, Jean Almicar, who became the pet of Marie Antoinette.[14]

Most of the published information on Ourika, like that in the 1874 *Revue historique, nobiliaire, et biographique*, comes from items about Boufflers and other members of the white aristocracy. So we know that "Charlotte-Catherine-Benezet-Ourika" accompanied the chevalier when he returned to France in August 1786 aboard *Le Rossignol*, which docked at La Rochelle. Boufflers arranged to have her baptized in Paris on 16 September.[15]

Even these details remain difficult to verify, and many writers seem to have relied on Duras's fiction to fill in those historical gaps. Roger Little, for example, writes about Ourika's life in France as if it were a fairy tale, an exceptional rags-to-riches narrative complete with happily-ever-after ending. In this version, Ourika was treated as a member of the Beauvau family, showered with "tenderness and love," and surrounded by the "brilliant salon" of her adopted family. Nothing appears to have been denied to her. According to Thérèse De Raedt, however, the chevalier gave Ourika to his uncle, M. de Beauvau, to repay him for his help in securing the Senegalese governorship. Little also writes of Ourika's "possible excessive fondness for her adopted brother," Juste de Noailles, and her lovesickness over him. Little then appears to take a step back, declaring, "a story is not History" (Une histoire n'est pas l'Histoire).[16]

Around 1793, when Beauvau died, Sophie de Tott (1758–ca. 1840) painted a portrait of Ourika (fig. 4).[17] Although the girl in the image is smiling and seems to be well cared for, the bracelets high on her arm and ankles and her single bare breast and bare feet sexualize her, referring the viewer to a type of Orientalist fantasy about Africa. The bracelets are reminiscent of slave shackles, and her non-Europeanness is emphasized by the contrast with the ornate furniture, her benefactor's white marble bust (he had been a member of the Société des amis des noirs), and the laurels she wears and is placing atop the bust.[18]

Anne Louise Germaine de Staël-Holstein, commonly known as Mme. de Staël, a close friend of Duras, also met Ourika in a salon and used her name for a character in *Mirza; ou, Lettre d'un voyageur* (1795). Another aristocrat, the Marquise de Henriette Lucie Dillon La Tour du Pin, whose memoirs chronicle a half century of life in France, wrote about spending time with the young Ourika. The memoirs offer some insight into Ourika's childhood and her status in Parisian social circles but also demonstrate the casual racism of the marquise. According to La Tour du Pin, "In the evening, we made music, accompanied by Mme. de Poix, who was an excellent musician, and Mme. la Maréchale was amused to see me create a tableau with her little negress Ourika. I took her on my lap, she wrapped her arms around my neck and pressed her little face, black as ebony, against my white cheek. Mme. de Beauvau never tired of this scene, which bored me greatly, because I always hated artificial things."[19] It is unclear exactly which part of the

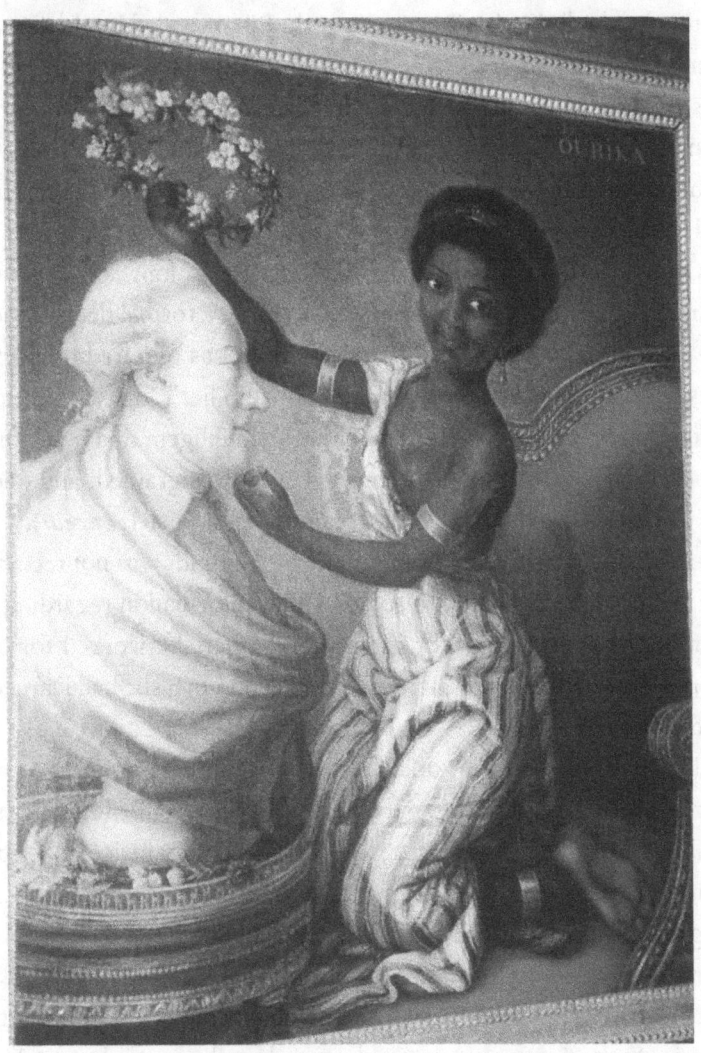

FIGURE 4.

Sophie de Tott (1758–ca. 1840), *Ourika*, ca. 1793.
The date of this painting and Ourika's apparent young age suggest that it may
have been rendered of her at an earlier age then she would have been in 1793.
Reproduced with permission from R. Little and the University of Exeter Press.

night she found so boring and artificial: the music or the display of affection by the little girl. Was La Tour du Pin offended by the fact that Ourika had the run of the room or that her mistress encouraged Ourika's physical proximity with her white friends? Was Ourika's "performance" in this space disconcerting? What is clear, however, is that La Tour du Pin sought to emphasize the contrast between her white cheek and Ourika's skin, "black as ebony."

On 15 December 1794, when she was about fourteen years old, Ourika "appeared before a notary... to make a formal declaration of her emancipation in front of seven witnesses, as required by law because her biological parents were unknown to her" (fig. 5). The court noted that "because she was known to be intelligent and a person of good morals," her request for emancipation was granted, and one of the witnesses, Jean Nicolas Deal, became her guardian (*curateur*).[20] She received an annuity, though the source of the funds was not recorded, but had no dowry. There is also no further information regarding her relationship with Deal—for example, whether she worked for him. Ourika signed the document herself, indicating that she had learned to read and write.

The only other extant document with Ourika's signature is a 28 March 1798 agreement (fig. 6). Historian Pierre Boulle finds this signature "particularly interesting," seeing signs of maturity in her penmanship: "The writing, though recognizable from the earlier one, no longer is that of a little school girl, but of someone who's developed her own mature identity."[21]

Less than a year later, Ourika died, probably of pneumonia or tuberculosis. At the time of her death, she was described as eighteen, single, and black, and she was buried at Saint-Germain-en-Laye on 19 January 1799. Her benefactors were subsequently revealed to have been Mme. de Beauvau; Pierre Chambert and his wife, Genevieve Marguerite Solly; and Antoine Arnoult Lavallard and his wife, Marie Antoinette Chambert.[22]

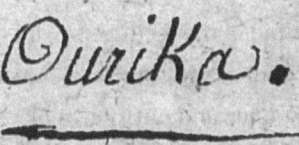

FIGURE 5.

Ourika's signature, taken from her declaration of emancipation, 15 December 1794.
This is one of only two surviving examples of her signature.
Courtesy of Archives de Paris.

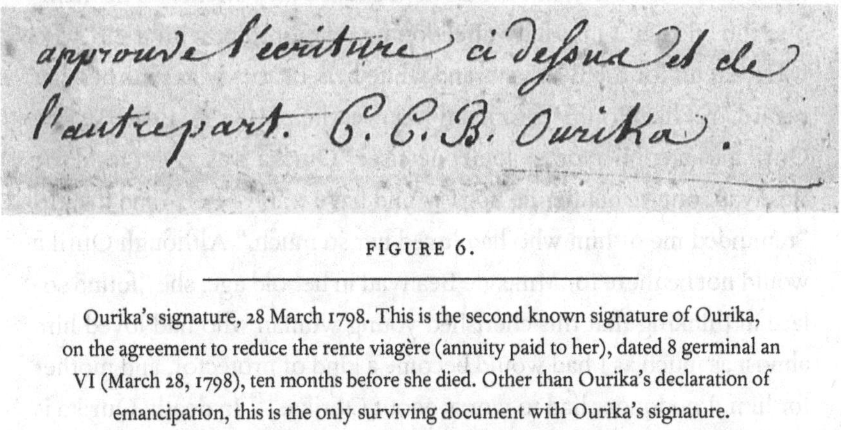

FIGURE 6.

Ourika's signature, 28 March 1798. This is the second known signature of Ourika,
on the agreement to reduce the rente viagère (annuity paid to her), dated 8 germinal an
VI (March 28, 1798), ten months before she died. Other than Ourika's declaration of
emancipation, this is the only surviving document with Ourika's signature.
Additionally, it demonstrates a development in Ourika's penmanship during the
four years between the signing of the two documents. Courtesy of Archives de Paris.

During Ourika's lifetime, the maréchal's affection for her appeared genuine, and his wife came to feel the same way. Nevertheless, Mme. de Beauvau's writing about the girl was condescending and displayed benign racism: Ourika "was born with great spirit, and the most remarkable quality of her mind was an accuracy and natural taste, which surprised me every time in the reading we did together. Her purity can only be compared to that of the Angels."[23] Mme. de Beauvau was "surprised" to find intelligence and purity in a black female body. Mme. de Beauvau also remarked on Ourika's "gentle and modest pride" and "natural propriety," pleasing figure, beautiful eyes, grace, and charm. But, she continued, Ourika's "color might have made us fear for her"—presumably a reference to her lack of marriage prospects had she lived.[24]

Mme. de Beauvau was deeply saddened at Ourika's passing, writing that "the death of my dear Ourika has been gentle as her life." Beauvau found a handwritten note in Ourika's wallet stating, "my mother and father abandoned me, but the Lord had taken pity on me." The memoirs thus depict a mutually affectionate relationship, with a girl who was grateful for the Beauvaus and white benefactors who returned her regard. Yet like Boufflers so many years earlier, Mme. de Beauvau saw Ourika as a connector to someone else: "Ourika was given to M. de Beauvau, or else neither he nor I would have wanted her," and the girl "reminded me of him who had loved her so much." Although Ourika would not be there for Mme. de Beauvau in her old age, she "found solace in thinking that this cherished young woman who had loved him almost as much as I had would become a kind of protector, and mother for him. I no longer had to worry about Ourika."[25] In death, Ourika is no longer a burden for Mme. de Beauvau and simultaneously becomes a guardian angel or mother for M. de Beauvau.

An anonymous painting of an older Ourika (fig. 7) shows a somber-looking young woman. There is no way to determine how this image relates to the happy child in Tott's painting. Was Ourika saddened by her removal from her home and by being "gifted" to strang-

FIGURE 7.

Anonymous, *Ourika*. This painting of Ourika as a young woman is likely the last depiction of her created during her lifetime.

ers half a world away? Did she feel genuine affection for her mistress? If Mme. de Beauvau's account is accurate, Ourika spent most of her life with people who cared for her and thought of her almost (but not quite) as family. Nevertheless, Boufflers forcefully removed her from her childhood home and her biological family, and her benefactors, the Beauvaus, always maintained some emotional distance. There is no way to determine whether she felt rescued, stolen, or some combination of the two. Ourika would have been no more than seven when Boufflers acquired her, meaning that she likely had few memories of her life before that time, though she evidently retained a feeling of abandonment. Is her sadness in this painting (like the one of her smiling earlier) not also a projection of the artists that depict her, marking her with their views on race and her life of belonging (or not belonging) in Paris? We may know little about Ourika both before and during her time in Parisian society, but she clearly played multiple roles in elite identity, serving as plaything, status symbol, rescuer, benefactor, confidant, and muse, often simultaneously.

SARAH BAARTMANN

Sarah Baartmann was born in South Africa, fifty miles north of the Gamtoos River, probably during the 1770s.[26] Little is known about Baartmann's life before her arrival in London in 1810, but she may already have been married and had children.[27] According to musicologist Percival Kirby, Baartmann was smuggled out of British-occupied Cape Town by Hendrik Cesars (the brother of her old master, Peter) without the colonial governor's knowledge.[28] They sailed from Cape Town on 7 April 1810 aboard the HMS *Diadem*, with Baartmann the only female on board, and arrived in Chatham, thirty miles from London, in July. At some point, Cesars entered into a partnership of sorts with surgeon Alexander Dunlop, who was notable for his penchant for exporting "museum specimens" from South Africa and who had first seen Baartmann in Cape Town around 1809. According to an alleged contract between the two men and Baartmann, she would perform domestic duties and be exhibited in England and Ireland, and a portion of her earnings would fund her repatriation to South Africa after two years.[29] Because she was considered an oddity, her handlers hoped that European fascination for certain types of human curiosities would garner income and fame.

The arrival in London of "the Hottentot," as Baartmann was known as early as her time in Cape Town, generated considerable public excitement (see fig. 8). For a small fee, spectators could enter an arena in which "a stage [was] raised about three feet from the floor, with a cage, or enclosed place at the end of it; ... the Hottentot was within the cage; [and] on being ordered by her keeper, she came out, and ... her appear-

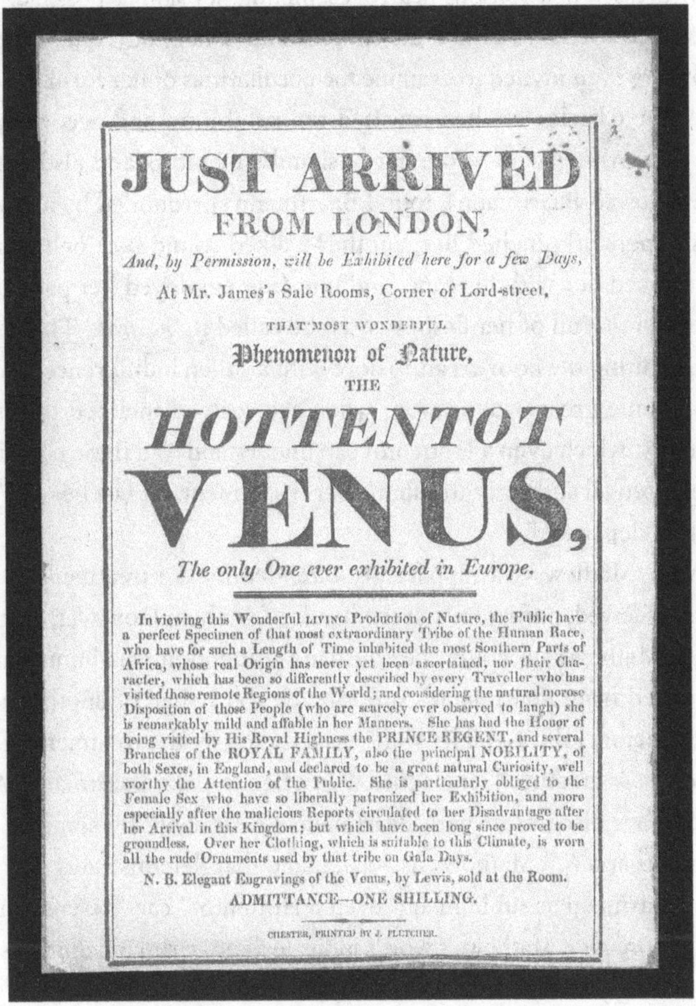

JUST ARRIVED
FROM LONDON,
And, by Permission, will be Exhibited here for a few Days,
At Mr. James's Sale Rooms, Corner of Lord-street,
THAT MOST WONDERFUL
Phenomenon of Nature,
THE
HOTTENTOT
VENUS,
The only One ever exhibited in Europe.

In viewing this Wonderful LIVING Production of Nature, the Public have a perfect Specimen of that most extraordinary Tribe of the Human Race, who have for such a Length of Time inhabited the most Southern Parts of Africa, whose real Origin has never yet been ascertained, nor their Character, which has been so differently described by every Traveller who has visited those remote Regions of the World; and considering the natural morose Disposition of those People (who are scarcely ever observed to laugh) she is remarkably mild and affable in her Manners. She has had the Honor of being visited by His Royal Highness the PRINCE REGENT, and several Branches of the ROYAL FAMILY, also the principal NOBILITY, of both Sexes, in England, and declared to be a great natural Curiosity, well worthy the Attention of the Public. She is particularly obliged to the Female Sex who have so liberally patronized her Exhibition, and more especially after the malicious Reports circulated to her Disadvantage after her Arrival in this Kingdom; but which have been long since proved to be groundless. Over her Clothing, which is suitable to this Climate, is worn all the rude Ornaments used by that tribe on Gala Days.

N. B. Elegant Engravings of the Venus, by Lewis, sold at the Room.

ADMITTANCE—ONE SHILLING.

CHESTER, PRINTED BY J. FLETCHER.

FIGURE 8.

Broadside advertising an appearance by the Hottentot Venus in Chester, England, ca. 1810. This advertisement demonstrates the manner in which Sarah Baartmann was perceived as a consumable commodity, able to be displayed and viewed by English society for the profit of her exhibitors.

ance was highly offensive to delicacy."[30] According to one official, she was "dressed in a color as nearly resembling her skin as possible. The dress is contrived to exhibit the entire frame of her body, and the spectators are even invited to examine the peculiarities of her form."[31]

Actor Charles Mathews visited the exhibition and according to his wife, Anne (who wrote her husband's memoirs and also apparently viewed Baartmann), found Baartmann surrounded by a crowd: "One [person] pinched her, another walked round her; one gentleman poked her with his cane, and one *lady* employed her parasol to ascertain that all of her flesh was, as she called it, '*nattral*.' This inhumane baiting the poor creature bore with a sullen indifference, except upon some great provocation, when she seemed inclined to resent brutality, which even a Hottentot can understand. On these occasions it required all authority to subdue her resentment. At last her *civilized* visitors departed."[32]

Anne Mathews was apparently offended by the treatment Baartmann received, particularly at the hands of women. However, according to Mathews's account, her husband's attention was immediately distracted from Baartmann's suffering by the arrival of another celebrated actor, John Kemble, who was shocked by the treatment of the "poor, *poor* creature!" and refused an offer to poke Baartmann. And despite her discomfort with Baartmann's treatment "by some of our own barbarians," Mathews uses language that demonstrates that she saw Baartmann as subhuman ("even a Hottentot" can "resent brutality.") Moreover, Mathews's words indicate that Baartmann did not submit willingly to this treatment, though it is not clear what sort of "authority" was needed to "subdue" her.[33]

Mathews also wrote about Baartmann's body: "In those days, when *bustles* were *not*, she was a curiosity, for English ladies then wore no shape but what Nature gave and insisted upon."[34] The Mathewses were both fascinated and repulsed by Baartmann, underscoring the power she was believed to exert over others, and Anne Mathews seems to have believed that at least on some level, Baartmann had control over her situation. The struggle for control over her body revolved around the outrageous spectacle of Baartmann on display and the remarkable ease of those who abused her.

In November 1810, Zachary Macaulay and other abolitionists began legal proceedings to determine whether she was being held against her will. Documents relating to what was aptly yet derogatively titled the Case of the Hottentot Venus highlight the contradictions surrounding her voyage to England and the ambiguous nature of her status, and speak to a strong need to represent Baartmann as an active and free agent in her own exhibition. According to the court documents, she was "perfectly happy in her present situation; had no desire whatever of returning to her own country, not even for the purpose of seeing her two brothers and four sisters." According to the record of her three-hour interrogation on 27 November 1810, Baartmann testified that she had made an agreement with Dunlop and had "personally" asked for permission to make the voyage. Moreover, the document asserted that she was happy and said she had "everything she wants," including two negro boys to wait on her. Her only complaint was the desire for warmer clothes.[35]

But Baartmann did not respond to the question of whether she could go back to Cape Hope at any time, and the validity of her testimony is challenged by the fact that she could not read or write (her first-person voice never appears in the text) and by the possibility that she spoke her African language and Dutch but not English. According to the transcript, "she understands very little of the Agreement made with her by Mr. Dunlop on the twenty ninth October 1810," so it is unclear how she could have corroborated its contents. Nevertheless, notary Arend Jacob Guitard signed an affidavit declaring that she wanted to be exhibited and that she said she was being treated well and wanted to stay in England. He also claimed that the agreement had been translated for her benefit (though he did not indicate by whom) and read to her numerous times and that he had questioned her directly.[36]

Macaulay and his fellow abolitionists painted a far different picture. They emphasized Baartmann's treatment while on exhibit and her demeanor—"morose, sullen, distressed, mortified, miserable, and degraded"—as evidence of her coercion. They stressed the parallels between her treatment and that of zoo animals and noted that her handler regularly threatened her so that she would perform. They also asserted that she refused to answer when questioned in Dutch about her condition, contradicting Guitard's account.[37] In short, the men who brought the court case seemed determined to prove that Baartmann needed to be freed from Cesars—that she was in fact enslaved.

Thus, efforts to make Baartmann appear a willing participant in her exploitation were crucial. If she were acting under her own free will, her treatment simply became part of a job to which she had lawfully, contractually, and voluntarily agreed, and those viewing her were absolved of any responsibility for the fact that she was being held in a cage and apparently forced to perform. But this battle to define her status overlooked the fact that the slave system operating in Africa and Great Britain meant that by definition, she could not possibly be acting under her own free will. It also negated the fact that she had been purchased as a slave before traveling to England.

The legal case was dismissed and ultimately only generated further attention to Baartmann and increased the popularity of her exhibitions. In 1811, she performed in Bath and in Manchester, where the Reverend Joshua Brookes baptized her on 7 December (fig. 9). The name on her baptismal certificate is not the Dutch *Saartje Baartmann* but the Anglicized *Sarah Bartmann*.[38]

Baartmann's trail subsequently becomes more difficult to follow. She is believed to have married while in England, though no documentary proof has been found. When Dunlop died in July 1812, Cesars's whereabouts were unknown. Baartmann was displayed in Ireland in 1812, and she apparently met up with traveling shows (and may have hired herself out to them) until Henry Taylor took her to France in 1814. She appeared on public display there, but little additional information is available about her time in Paris prior to her death there as a result of tuberculosis or smallpox in late December 1815 or early January 1816.[39]

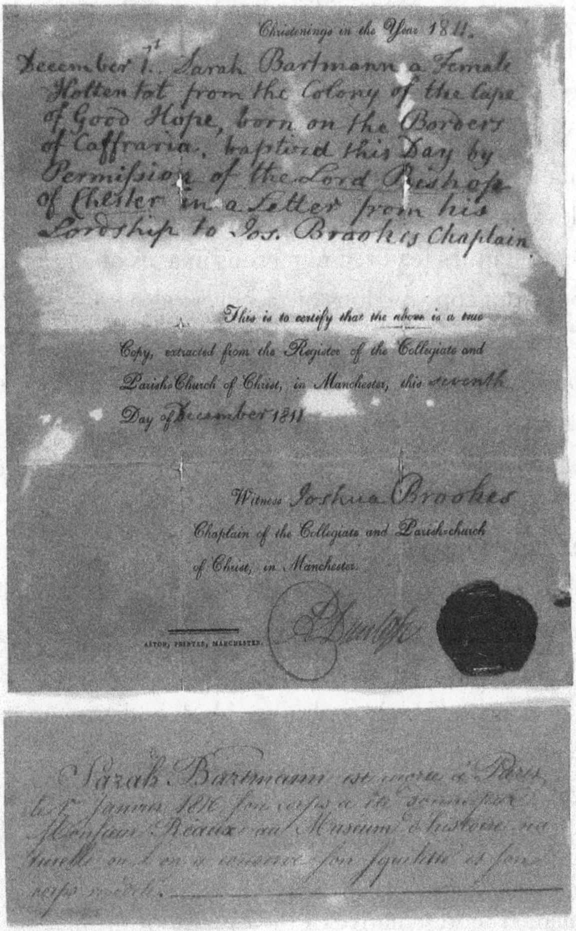

Christenings in the Year 1811.

December 7th. Sarah Bartmann a Female Hottentot from the Colony of the Cape of Good Hope, born on the Borders of Caffraria, baptized this Day by Permission of the Lord Bishop of Chester in a Letter from his Lordship to Jos. Brookes Chaplain

This is to certify that the above is a true Copy, extracted from the Register of the Collegiate and Parish-Church of Christ, in Manchester, this seventh Day of December 1811

Witness Joshua Brookes
Chaplain of the Collegiate and Parish-church of Christ, in Manchester.

AITON, PRINTER, MANCHESTER.

Sarah Bartmann est morte à Paris le 1er Janvier 1816 son corps a été donné par Monsieur Réaux au Muséum d'histoire naturelle où l'on a conservé son squelette et son corps moulé.

FIGURE 9.

Sarah Baartmann's baptismal certificate, 7 December 1811. The folds in the paper indicate that it had been opened and reopened on numerous occasions, which suggests that the document had meaning (or usefulness) for her. Reproduced with permission from Muséum national d'histoire naturelle, Paris.

In the eighteenth and nineteenth centuries, the empirical knowledge provided by scientific study increasingly became a way to make sense of France's many distressing political and cultural reorganizations, including their own society, people around the world, nature, and the human body. Long-standing discussions about race merged with these studies. As scientific communities, particularly in France and Germany, sought to evaluate and classify all people, including people of African descent, medical journals, conferences, anthropological studies, and legal statutes featured numerous images of and references to black people. But constructions of race were also informed by gender roles.[40] The guise of "impartial" scientific rhetoric helped to naturalize opinions about acceptable societal boundaries, and the spectacle of Sarah Baartmann in Paris allowed scientists to manipulate data to solidify already held beliefs. Developing racial hierarchies served as justification for colonial occupation and imperial domination. These scientists perpetuated the notion that body size and shape correlated to intelligence and social roles, making those peoples (and their bodies) inferior to whites (and their definitions of ideal beauty and proper social roles). Scientists altered and even falsified data to perpetuate the idea that Baartmann's body and other black bodies were inferior to those of whites.

In his discussion of the iconography of female sexuality in the nineteenth century, Sander Gilman writes, "While many groups of African blacks were known to Europeans in the nineteenth century, the Hottentot remained representative of the essence of the black, especially the black female."[41] Gilman posits that the Hottentot Venus "served as the emblem of black sexuality during the entire nineteenth century, a sexuality inherently different from that of the European."[42] T. Denean Sharpley-Whiting concurs, stating that the Hottentot Venus exerted an "immense influence on nineteenth-century Western racial-sexual science."[43] Enlightenment ideology was based on the dominant hierarchy of the lowest to highest in anthropologist Christian Meiners's "chain of being," and aesthetics constituted an important factor in determining how these placements could be understood. George Mosse contends that in the eighteenth century, anthropologists considered Hottentot Africans among the lowliest "creatures" in the link between animals and humans.[44] Within William Cheselden's perception theory and other eighteenth-century European debates regarding blackness, German dramatist and critic Gotthold Ephraim Lessing's aesthetic theory consolidated and provided a template for linking "ultimate filth," aesthetics, and blackness into a single but far-reaching archetype: Hottentot Africans. If Greeks provided the ultimate eighteenth-century standard of beauty, Hottentot Africans provided the repugnant antithesis.

Popular ideas of racial inferiority received legitimacy via placement within a "scientific" context. Joanna De Groot posits that

> the founding of learned societies, journals, and academic institutions for medicine, anthropology, geography, and linguistic studies brought the study of human characteristics, differences, or cultures firmly into the sphere of science, rationality, and professional expertise. . . . This is by no means the only or even the most powerful source of images of "sex" or "race," but it certainly constituted one of the most authoritative and influential ways of grounding the "Otherness" of femininity or ethnic identity in "real" knowledge wielded by prestigious professionals (doctors, academics, "experts").[45]

While eighteenth-century scientists believed that environment made blacks inferior, nineteenth-century science emphasized race itself as the cause of black inferiority. Moreover, because race was biologically determined, inferiority was an inherent characteristic. As Europeans observed Baartmann and discussed her supposed inferiority or ugliness, they constantly reevaluated and reworked those conversations.

However, the obsession with the "Hottentot African" ran the risk of also generating desire: one covets what one sees. To protect the viewer's identity and objectivity, the gaze must be narrowly focused and specifically directed—explained as a means of identification and classification, nothing more. According to Gilman, "To meet . . . scientific standards, a paradigm was needed which would technically place both the sexuality and the beauty of the black in an antithetical position to that of the white."[46] Baartmann became extremely useful in this effort. By attributing her body to a racial characteristic, she became a scientific specimen.[47] But as imagery of and discussions about her show, white Frenchmen did not always succeed in creating these boundaries.

Scientists' alleged expertise enabled them to express themselves in an idiom that laypeople perceived as objective and thus provided cover for interest in sexual matters that would otherwise have been unacceptable. The genitals of black women could be studied as a means to uncover and reinforce the unchanging nature of blacks and their sexual uncontrollability, which, in turn, could then be used to understand other forms of sexual pathology. Understanding the Hottentot Venus might enable scientists to understand black sexuality and sexual desire as a whole, and the medical establishment rapidly began to conflate the "abnormality" of black sexuality with disease: as Gilman writes, "When, in the late nineteenth century, medical literature likened the genitalia of the black female to those of the infected prostitute, the fear (and fascination) accompanying the one became associated with the other."[48]

Baartmann's death thus offered a tremendous opportunity for Georges Léopold Cuvier, whom Napoleon had appointed surgeon general in 1812.[49] The French royalist newspaper *La Quotidienne* announced on 1 January 1816, "The Hottentot Venus is dead this morning after an illness of three days. It is said that the professors of the Museum of Natural History have asked for her body to be turned over to them."[50] Indeed, Cuvier had requested and received permission from the police to obtain Baartmann's cadaver so that he could dissect and examine it. He not only made a plaster cast of her body (fig. 10) but dissected her buttocks and pickled her brain and genitals, storing them in jars as specimens.

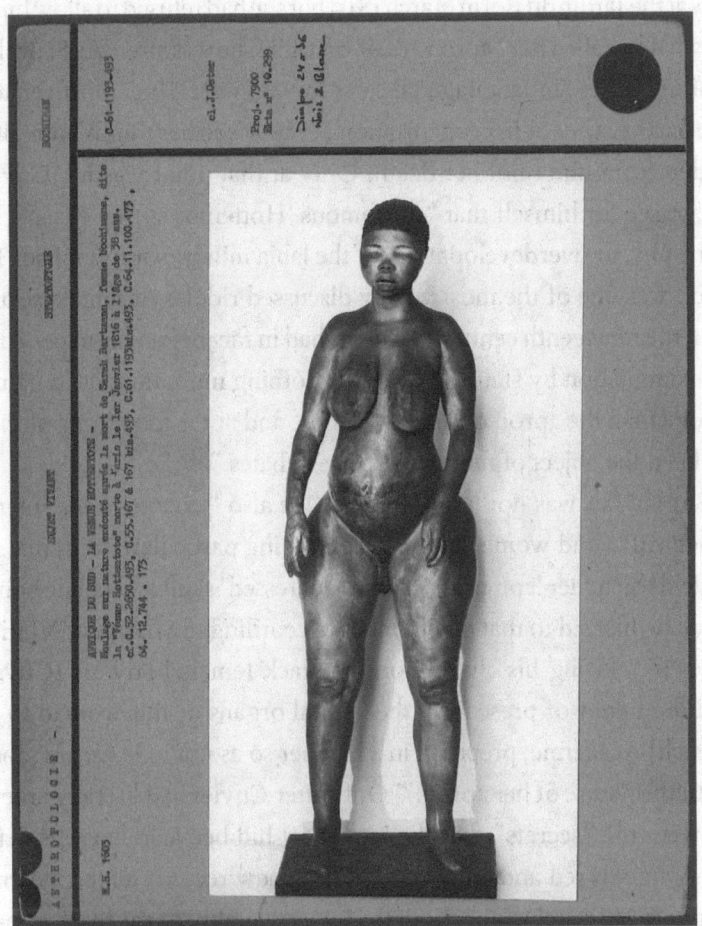

FIGURE 10.

Sarah Baartmann's body cast, 1816. The cast was made of Baartmann's body after she died, but given the manipulation of her body in life, there is no certainty that Cuvier did not continue that distortion after death by altering the cast.
© Musée du Quai Branly–Jacques Chirac, Paris.

Baartmann's genitals were the real prize of Cuvier's anatomical dissection. He had arranged to have her sketched and examined for three days at the Jardin du Roi in March 1815, but she had refused to allow him to see what he called her "apron" (*tablier*) while she was alive. As Sharpley-Whiting notes (in language taken from Cuvier): The "most remarkable particularity of her organization . . . between her thighs" remained hidden from him until her death. Only at that point was he [Cuvier] able to see for himself that "the famous 'Hottentot apron' [was] a hypertrophy, or overdevelopment, of the labia minora, or nymphae. The apron was one of the most widely discussed riddles of female sexuality in the nineteenth century." Cuvier had in fact begun his paper about the examination by stating, "There is nothing more famous in natural history than the apron of the Hottentots, and at the same time nothing has been the object of more numerous debates."[51]

But Cuvier was not finished there. He also "examined the interior of her vulva and womb, and finding nothing particularly different, he move[d] on to her 'compressed' and 'depressed' skull and pelvic bone," which he likened to that of a monkey. According to Sharpley-Whiting, "In 1816, closing his chapter on the black female body, he [Cuvier] 'had the honor of presenting the genital organs of this woman to the [French] Académie, prepared in a manner so as not to leave any doubt about the nature of her apron.'" Only after Cuvier had literally entered her were the "secrets" that the Hottentot hid between her legs definitively uncovered and analyzed.[52] These new records added a certain weight to his conclusions about the hypersexuality of the black female.

Cuvier compared Baartmann with European women, particularly highlighting the difference in sex organs. Because Baartmann's genitalia were supposedly closer to those of a monkey than to those of European women, the latter were elevated. Henri de Blainville, who had joined Cuvier in observing Baartmann, also published his findings. Fausto-Sterling writes that Baartmann "drank, smoked, and was alleged to be sexually aggressive" (something that Blainville states he is uncertain about), all stereotypically masculine characteristics. Despite comparing Baartmann to an orangutan, however, Cuvier also conceded, notes Anne Fausto-Sterling, that "she spoke several languages, had a good ear for music, and possessed a good memory" even though "her physiognomy—her face—repelled him."[53] Cuvier's account reveals that she clearly fascinated him in ways that went beyond his scientific authority and exceeded his preconceived notions of black women.

Cuvier's and other scientists' notes and diagrams of Baartmann allow us to interrogate the scientists' findings, sometimes in ways they might not have expected. For example, X-rays of Baartmann's skull and brain taken at the Jardin des Plantes around 2000 show that her brain was not substantially smaller than the average white subject's, especially when her stature is taken into account. In addition, Cuvier's wax models of Baartmann's genitalia do not reveal the deformities he so trumpeted in his autopsy of her. All of this suggests that he used "objective" science to suit his purposes of reaffirming the black body as inherently inferior on the level of human biology. That subsequent scientists and writers utilized Cuvier's falsified data and incorrect conclusions as the basis for more than a century of incorrect "scientific" discourse indicates what was at stake in this discussion of the black female body and its inferiority to the white female body.

Fausto-Sterling points out that "Cuvier most clearly concerned himself with establishing the priority of European nationhood; he wished to control the hidden secrets of Africa and the woman by exposing them to scientific daylight."[54] In addition, Cuvier asserted French power to know the Other, thereby helping to further legitimize France's colonial project. Cuvier "proved" the Otherness of Sarah Baartmann, showed her as a deformed being, and reasserted European white male scientific dominance over both white and black women. The superiority of (male) whiteness was proved within and outside of the academy. It is thus particularly relevant that the only word we have a direct record of Baartmann saying is *No* in response to Cuvier's request to access her genitals and that the word was recorded by Cuvier himself in his account of her autopsy. Though Baartmann was manipulated while alive and then violated in death, when she refused to allow Cuvier total access to her body, he had no choice but to capitulate, however reluctantly.

JEANNE DUVAL

As is the case for Ourika and Baartmann, many of the details about Jeanne Duval's life are the product of hearsay, at times both vague and contradictory. Duval is best known as the common-law wife of Charles Baudelaire, a white French poet and icon, and her claim to fame (or infamy) came from Baudelaire's literary writings describing her as his "Vénus noire" and his copious letters about her. The 1857 publication of his *Les Fleurs du mal*, a poetic cycle in which numbers 22–39 are influenced by or about her, forever bound her to him. The book was quickly condemned on grounds of obscenity.

Duval is believed to have been born around 1820 in France and has been associated with several surnames, including *Prosper* as well as *Lemer* and *Lemaire*. In addition, she often performed under the stage name *Berthe*. Her grandmother, Marie Duval, may have been from Saint-Domingue and been of African descent.[55] Jeanne's mother, whose name may have been Jeanne-Marie-Marthe Duval, Jeanne Lemaire, or Jeanne Lemer, was "an old, respectable looking negress, with thick, greasy hair which tried in vain to twirl over her cheeks and ears," and is generally considered to have had ties to Nantes, although it is not clear whether she immigrated there or was born there. She may have been a prostitute, and both Jeanne Duval's father and grandfather were almost certainly white Frenchmen, though it is not known whether they were planters, slave owners, or members of the working class, and as far as the documents indicate, she had no contact with either man.[56]

Baudelaire's portrayal of Duval in his writings reflected not only his viewpoint but also his agenda. Baudelaire never married anyone else and enjoyed (if this is the correct word) a rather complicated relationship with his mother. In 1852, a decade after he first met Duval, Baudelaire declared of her, "Once she had certain qualities, but she has lost them, and I myself have gained insight. TO LIVE WITH A PERSON who never shows any gratitude for your efforts, who thwarts them by being clumsy or deliberately spiteful, who only considers you as her servant, and her property, with whom it is impossible to exchange one word on politics or literature, a creature WHO DOES NOT ADMIRE ME, and who is not even interested in my studies, who would throw my manuscripts into the fire if that would bring her more money than publishing them."[57] Baudelaire clearly sought to position Duval as duplicitous, stupid, and greedy so that he appeared as her opposite.

But such writings do offer some sense of the contours of Duval's life. Duval's existence was not only precarious but for more than two decades was entwined with Baudelaire's. They served as each other's lovers, enemies, friends, and caretakers. She was not merely a passive receptacle but an active participant in her own life and an integrated partner in his—because they chose to be with one another. Moreover, her relationship with him brought her into contact with such noted writers and artists as Honoré de Balzac, Maxime du Camp, Charles Toubin, Théophile Gautier, Gonzague de Reynold, Gustave Courbet, Théodore de Banville, Ernest Prarond, and Honoré Daumier, among others. In addition, Duval was also the mistress of one of the most prolific photographers of the nineteenth century, Gaspard-Félix Tournachon, also known as Nadar (1820–1910), although no photograph of her survives in his archive. Duval's associations with Baudelaire and Nadar meant that she was often surrounded by people of a different race and higher social class than her own.

Despite the fact that Duval was the companion of one of the most important writers in French history and was well known in nineteenth-century Paris's bohemian circles, there is virtually no record of her life aside from the reactions and opinions of famous white men. Thus, attempts to understand and contextualize her are difficult and potentially hazardous, since the descriptions reflect the observers' perspectives at least as much as Duval's reality.

Twentieth- and twenty-first-century black women artists and fiction writers have featured Duval in their works in an attempt to give her a voice, to make her exist in her own right in the realm of Baudelaire rather than to exist solely via others' representations.[58] Yet such attempts often reflect modern anger, sorrow, and voice, merely substituting a more sympathetic viewpoint for Baudelaire's lens on Duval's life. She remains a metaphor, a stand-in. But what does the more objective historical record actually tell us? The records offer multiple hints that she maintained a relationship with her mother until her death when Duval was an adult woman. Duval thus had a family beyond one famous white Frenchman as well as a career, albeit a sporadic one.

Duval's first documented appearance occurs in 1838, when she was in her late teens and Nadar saw her performing as an actress under the name *Mlle. Berthe* at Paris's Théâtre du Panthéon. At the time, acting was one of the few professions open to women with little education and particularly to women such as Duval who lacked traditional white families and the networks they provided that were essential for employment and marriage. As Elizabeth Wilson notes, however, acting "was an ambiguous profession for a woman in the mid-nineteenth century," and Duval is "invariably written off as a prostitute." Bourgeois anxieties about counterfeiting emotions for cash were a long-standing trope that linked theater and prostitution: Rousseau, for example, had in the eighteenth century criticized theater women as prostitutes, and Lenard Berlanstein calls acting a "deviant path" for women of Duval's era.[59] Her racial Othering thus intersected with gendered fears about emotional inauthenticity.

Duval's acting career continued at least intermittently for most of the next decade. In 1838–39, Berthe played the role of La Comtesse in *Rose et Colas; ou, Une Pièce de Sedaine*, a vaudeville in two acts, at the Théâtre de la Porte Saint-Antoine. She performed as "Thérèse: Domestique de la maison" (apparently with only one line) in *Le Système de mon oncle* on 2 December 1838.[60]

Duval again appeared in *Le Système de mon oncle* in 1840, and in 1842 she was performing at the Théâtre du Panthéon when, according to most biographers, Charles Baudelaire first saw her in an extremely minor part in a minor play: her only words were purportedly, "Dinner is served, Madame."[61] Their relationship continued for the rest of his life. By the end of October 1843, Duval lived with her mother at 6 rue de la Femme-sans-Tête, where she presumably tended Baudelaire when he was ill, though his primary residence was the Hôtel de Pimodan. From the hotel, he first mentioned Duval in an 1843 letter to his mother: "Do come now, *come immediately*—no prudishness. I am with a woman, and I am ill and I cannot move."[62] By the early 1840s, Baudelaire and Duval appeared together in public, frequenting "Daumier's digs on the rue de l'Hirondelle."[63]

Duval obtained her next known acting job in September 1844, when she appeared at the Théâtre de Belleville. The same year, according to Claude Pichois, "a mysterious Jeanne" and "her comrades from the Théâtre du Panthéon" demanded money that the director owed them. Pichois believes that this woman was Duval. She performed again in August and September 1845 at the Théâtre Beaumarchais (formerly Porte Saint-Antoine). In June 1845, Baudelaire attempted suicide with a knife while sitting next to Duval in a Paris café, requesting that she deliver a suicide note to his financial adviser, Narcisse Désiré Ancelle: "When Mademoiselle Jeanne Lemer brings you this letter, I will be dead." Baudelaire's letters suggest that both he and Duval struggled financially, and it is possible that the suicide attempt was intended to persuade Ancelle to provide them with money. Whatever the case, in January 1846, she performed again at the Théâtre Beaumarchais.[64]

From August until July 1847, Duval stayed with Baudelaire in Neuilly, not far from Ancelle, and they traveled together that October to Chateauroux. In 1850, Baudelaire visited Dijon, where Duval joined him.

In March 1853, Baudelaire wrote to his mother:

> A year ago I left Jeanne, as I told you,—although you doubted the truth of this, a fact that caused me pain.... For several months, I went to see her two or three times a month, to take her a little money. Well, now she is gravely ill, and in the direst poverty. I never speak of it to *Ancelle*. The wretch would be only too delighted at such news. It's obvious that a small portion of the money you send me will go to her. Now I'm annoyed I've said that since you're capable, in your heavy-handed maternal way, of sending her money, without telling me, through M. Ancelle. That would be extremely improper. You don't want to wound me again, do you? That idea is now going to swell and root itself in my brain, and persecute me.[65]

In November of that year, Duval's mother died, and Baudelaire paid for her funeral and burial at Belleville Cemetery, though he, too, continued to have financial problems.[66]

Duval and Baudelaire apparently reconciled at some point, briefly separated again beginning in December 1854, and then resumed their relationship in January 1855, when they were living at 18 rue d'Angoulême-du-Temple. In September 1856, however, he wrote, "My liaison, my liaison of fourteen years with Jeanne, is broken."[67]

By February 1859, Duval had moved to 22 rue Beautreillis, where Baudelaire joined her in March and remained for about six weeks. On 5 April, she suffered a stroke and was cared for at La Maison municipale de santé (the workhouse hospital) on rue du Faubourg Saint-Dénis. According to hospital records, she was "32 years old; without profession; single; living on rue Beautreilly [sic], 22, born in Saint Domingue. Room 8. Entered [the hospital] 5 April, left 15 May 1859." In May, while she was still in the hospital, her leg became paralyzed.[68] In reality, almost none of this information (her marital status, employment, or birthplace) was correct.

In 1860–61, Duval lived at 4 rue Louis-Philippe in Neuilly. Baudelaire lived with her for some of that time; at other times, she lived there with a man alleged to be her brother, though there is no record that she had a brother and her relationship with that man deepened the discord between her and Baudelaire. They split again in February 1861, and in March, Baudelaire wrote that Duval had asked someone "to buy some books and drawings from her. . . . It is all one to me, if she chooses to sell souvenirs which every man leaves with a woman he has lived with for years, but I had the humiliation of having to supply my publisher with vague explanations."[69]

At the first of April, Baudelaire reported to his mother that Duval "came to me yesterday. She's just left the hospice and her brother, whom I believed to be supporting her, sold in her absence part of her furniture. She's going to sell the rest to pay off a few debts." Though Baudelaire never saw her again, he remained preoccupied with her, and in May 1861, he wrote, "Jeanne will go into a nursing-home, where only what is strictly necessary will be paid. . . . From the beginning of next year, I shall consecrate to Jeanne the income of what capital remains. She will retire somewhere so as not to be completely alone. . . . In four months, since my flight from Neuilly, I have given her seven francs." Three years later, Baudelaire wrote to Ancelle, "I beg you to send 50 francs in an envelope to Jeanne (address: Jeanne Prosper, 17, rue Sauffroy Batignolles). . . . I believe that this unfortunate Jeanne has gone blind." In 1865, Baudelaire drew her from memory. Two years later, shortly before his death on 31 August 1867 of complications of syphilis and alcoholism, he dedicated one of his works "À Mlle B.," which may have been a discreet reference using her former stage name.[70] Baudelaire's words clearly demonstrate that whatever anger he felt toward Duval was also accompanied by caring, and for the rest of his life, he refused to completely abandon his ill former lover. However, he also had Courbet erase her from an 1854–55 painting, *L'Atelier du peintre* (see fig. 17, p. 106).[71]

Duval outlived her former lover and continued to interact with their bohemian social circle even as her health further deteriorated. Nadar claims he saw Duval for the last time in 1870, when she was on crutches. Singer Emma Calvé visited with Duval sometime between 1870 and 1878, when she was living

> under the name Jeanne Prosper . . . she lived in a modest abode, somewhere in Batignolles.
>
> We were ushered into a stuffy yellow room.
>
> She arrived shortly after, leaning on two crutches, wearing a madras turban from which wild, gray, curly locks and gold earrings escaped.
>
> She must have been nearing sixty but retained a golden complexion and beautiful eyes, of which Baudelaire said, "She has beautiful, soft, and nostalgic eyes that seem to long for the absent coconut palm." . . .
>
> "You must have been glorious to have been loved by such a great writer?"
>
> "Yes," she said, straightening up. "Ah! He really loved me. He was always a beautiful lover, so gentle with me, but not funny, always sad with . . . fantasies of another world."
>
> And with a sigh:
>
> "I do not wish for you to be loved by a poet, my beauties, even if he was the greatest of all."
>
> Then she pulled out a box of letters, from which she read us some passages, but she did not allow us to touch them. "These are my relics," she said. "I sold some of them, as I am not rich, but these here, the first ones and the last ones that he wrote me, will follow me into the coffin!"[72]

According to Calvé, Duval was wearing a madras head covering, more typical of the colonies than of France itself, and seemed to be longing for the tropics—the coconut palm. Yet nothing else in the contemporary writings about or visual depictions of Duval locates her in a colonial setting. This black Frenchwoman living in mid-nineteenth-century France represents the conflation of French, African, and Haitian identities. Though she spent her entire life in France, her contemporaries portrayed her as inauthentic—a representation that persists in scholarly literature to the present. Not only have the box and its contents disappeared, so has she. Though she is believed to have died shortly after her meeting with Calvé, Jeanne Duval's exact date of death and place of burial are unknown.[73]

CONCLUSION

The fragmentary nature of the information regarding the lives of Ourika, Sarah Baartmann, and Jeanne Duval makes telling their stories challenging. But at the same time, the fact that they left any traces at all makes these scraps tremendously powerful and the historical erasure of these narratives even more poignant.

Anne McClintock writes that commodity racism, which displaced the more elite scientific racism in England after 1850, reveals how fetishism is integral to European modernity, the metropole, and empire and that "commodity jingoism itself helped reinvent and maintain British national unity in the face of deepening imperial competition and colonial resistance."[74] But in France, this shift was fostered by the First Empire and occurred much earlier in the nineteenth century. As a racial commodity, Sarah Baartmann and her blackness were first consumed in more privatized spheres (as elites paid to see her) before moving to a larger-scale mass consumption through plays, letters (real and faked for consumer consumption), and other forms of consumer culture. The popular fascination with Baartmann constituted a response to the empire's collapse and a means of reestablishing that power and military prowess back home in the form of a black and spectacular totem. By the time Baartmann came around, the French expressed their anxiety by making a bigger spectacle of her and disguising it as entertainment. With Jeanne Duval, that social and cultural anxiety was complete: she was a living, breathing black Frenchwoman. Those tropes should no longer apply. But they do.

These women's real counterparts were culturally devoured, sliced, paraded, swallowed, and finally spit out as fantastical representations that bore scant resemblance to the originals. The French need for diversion transformed Baartmann, Ourika, and Duval into new and important types of fetishes for white men and women in France proper, far from the taint of colonies that France no longer unyieldingly and steadfastly commanded. The remainder of this book focuses on fictional productions of these women.

CHAPTER TWO

ENTERING DARKNESS

COLONIAL ANXIETIES AND THE CULTURAL PRODUCTION OF SARAH BAARTMANN

> De son image, en vain j'ai voulu me distraire.
> (In vain, I tried to free myself from her image.)
>
> —Observation regarding *La Vénus hottentote; ou, Haine aux françaises*, from the *Journal des débats et des décrets*, November 21, 1814 (quoting from Jean Racine's *Britannicus* [1669])

French painter Louis Léopold Boilly exhibited his *Les Galeries du Palais-Royal* (fig. 12) at the 1809 salon. Scholar Carol S. Eliel finds the painting, which features a motley crew of prostitutes, eager customers, dogs, bunnies, and onlookers standing underneath the galleries of the royal palace, a curious choice for such a venue.[1] Most of the men shop the wares of the young women, openly touching and inspecting them. None of the women appear to be smiling, save one—the black woman who is third from the right. The inclusion of the black woman, whom N. E. Rétif de la Bretonne names Esther in his writings about Paris life, is remarkable; the fact that her arms are wrapped around a white woman and a white boy is even more noteworthy.[2] She is close to the other racialized body in the image, an Arab-looking man who stares salaciously at the two women's breasts. The young white woman pets a

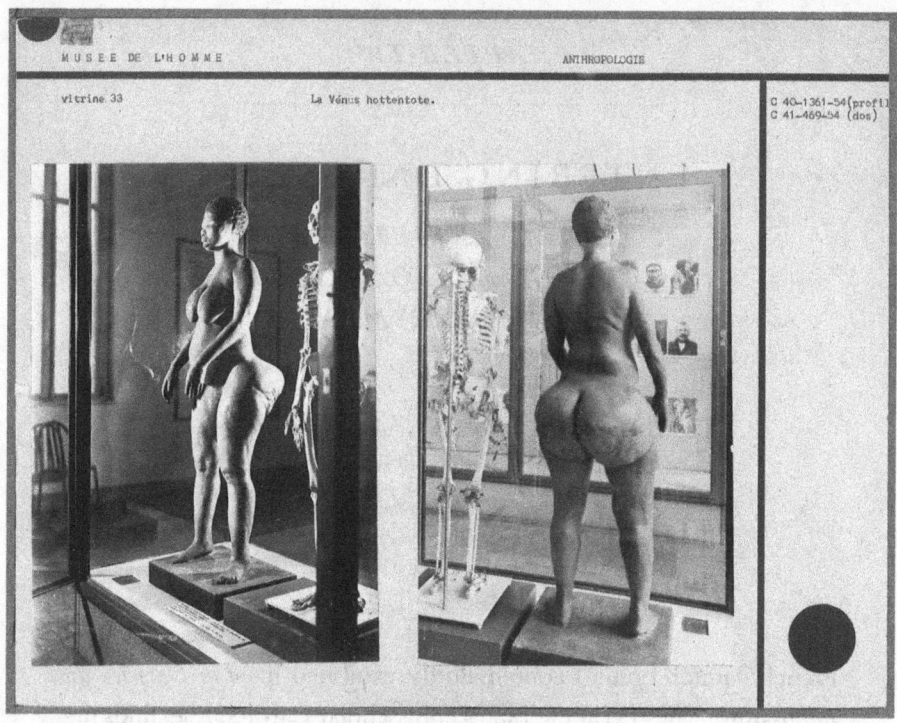

FIGURE 11.

"La Vénus hottentote" (body cast of Sarah Baartmann), vitrine 33, antropologie, courtesy of © musée du quai Branly–Jacques Chirac, Paris, France. For a number of years (until about the 1970s), visitors would see this image, which reflects the view of Baartmann as a scientific specimen, upon visiting the museum. Baartmann's brain, skeleton, and genitalia were repatriated in 2001 to South Africa, where she was properly buried.

FIGURE 12.

Louis-Léopold Boilly (1761–1845), *Galeries du Palais-Royal*, 1809.
The grouping of three on the right includes a black female prostitute.
Musée Carnavalet–Histoire de Paris, Paris.

rabbit in a box, unaware that the little boy may be using the animal as a ruse to get closer to her body as they are enfolded in Esther's embrace. Although many of the women have some head coverings of some kind, only Esther wears a tignon and jewelry, marking her blackness.

Esther is one of many prostitutes in the painting but is distinguished by her race and her class.[3] Her presence adds additional tension to the debauchery, further indicating a scene of questionable female behavior and misbelonging. In fact, de la Bretonne did not depict Esther in the frontispiece to his book, on which Boilly based his painting, an omission that Eliel suggests may have occurred because her presence was "too shocking for the public of 1790."[4] Prostitution may have been commonplace, but a black woman moved the image into a much more problematic space. Boilly's painting encapsulates both the scattered presence of black women in France and their association with sexual deviancy. The cultural use of black women to depict issues such as prostitution or illegitimacy was even more valuable when black women appeared to be coming into France in larger numbers (although they were not) and when issues of colonial failure aligned with tropes about black female bodies.

The story of Sarah Baartmann allows us to further explore how a black woman became such a potent cultural commodity. Baartmann was unique for the way in which her body became a scientific artifact, providing multiple benefits for white Frenchmen and -women: authoritative European male expertise; an opportunity for returning émigrés, colonial refugees, and commoners to observe anti-Frenchness via the spectacle of Baartmann and shore up their own identities; and the elevation of European womanhood through the demotion of the black female body. Baartmann provided a canvas on which others could paint an alternative history to the loss of empire and reflect a new collective public identity. Fictional literary texts that purported to represent Baartmann's voice and visual representations of her life in France demonstrate how depictions of black women were used to articulate these French anxieties and influenced debates concerning French national identity. As a black woman, Baartmann had to be controlled in a specific way because of her presence in France proper and because the wounds of the recent Haitian Revolution had not yet healed.

RACE, REVOLUTION, AND REPERCUSSIONS

Napoleon Bonaparte crowned himself emperor on 2 December 1804, leading to the return of those émigré nobles who had dispersed after the fall of Louis XVI. By the time he abdicated in April 1814, he had reestablished slavery (along with ancien régime slave laws) in all of France's black colonies. The next few years brought much political turmoil with the return of the Bourbon Dynasty under Louis XVIII, Napoleon's brief return between 20 March and 18 June 1815, and finally his defeat at Waterloo, which brought Louis XVIII back to the throne. The members of the French royalty were reestablished as the legitimate heirs to the throne, and the country rallied behind its new king during the Restoration, which lasted until 1830.

Political and social uncertainty marked this era, with royalists, Bonapartists, and republicans failing to reconcile their disparate ideologies. Historians generally agree that the Restoration saw enormous cultural and political changes that ultimately destabilized social markers such as gender, sexuality, and class.[5] One major capstone of French royal identity was its empire, and the return to royalism raised questions about the impact of the Haitian Revolution and particularly its racial ramifications.[6] Nevertheless, as William Cohen demonstrates, the Restoration monarchy not only remained "committed to colonial slavery and therefore continued the system of racial discrimination thought to be the necessary underpinning of slavery" but also actively promoted scholarship that supported slavery and censored those who preached abolition.[7] At the same time, other elites articulated racialized discourses on national identity to consolidate their own social control. Slavery and empire thus remained two of the few political, economic, and cultural constants between the seventeenth and mid-nineteenth centuries, a time when "French identity" was repeatedly redefined as a consequence of political turmoil and the end of the French Empire.

SARAH BAARTMANN'S ARRIVAL IN EUROPE

When Sarah Baartmann arrived in Paris in September 1814, she provided a convenient distraction from political upheaval and social change. Little work was required for Frenchmen and -women to see the "Hottentot Venus" as anything but the antithesis of French citizenship and civilization.[8] French laypeople joined this discourse through literature, plays, photography, art, and other cultural productions that offered an entry point for the members of the French bourgeoisie to contemplate the black Other and to raise their own collective self-esteem. That commodity was then reproduced for the masses. The French appropriated Baartmann's voice and body into a series of letters, a play, and other misrepresentations that repackaged and sold her as an important reminder (perhaps even a cautionary tale) for returning aristocratic émigrés and newly arrived colonial refugees. This image functioned within cultural and racial hierarchies to justify French expansion. Furthermore, her availability to be viewed meant that her body could be used (either for fantasy or as substitute to articulate those fantasies) without any sense of accountability. She seemed to invite the gaze even as she allegedly repelled the viewer—flagrant public seminudity, which she was said to have endorsed, provided proof of her corruption. Baartmann was a living, breathing embodiment of difference, both "scientifically" and in popular culture. Plays, periodicals, and artistic renderings displayed her as overtly sexualized and highlighted her racial and gender differences. Hypervisible and hypersexualized, she was viewed in different settings in accordance with class standing: the upper classes had the option of paying to view her privately, while the middle and working classes could view her only in more public settings.

White men's obsession with regaining a sense of control in the colonies became an attempt to control who belonged in France and who the French were now, an effort that required understanding and regulating bodies in France proper. The male-centered narrative of a New France was rooted in nostalgic (re)memberings and colonial fantasies that enabled white Frenchmen to mitigate the loss of the colonies and circumvent the reason for those losses. In addition, this strategy of cultural distraction allowed the policing of white women's bodies.

In these fictive portrayals of Baartmann, France's national identity was natural, while black identity was not. In fact, the two were incompatible, with blacks functioning as a type of pollutant, the epitome of the degenerate and deviant Other. The display of the Hottentot Venus in conversation with both white men and white women highlighted gender and racial differences. If the goddess Venus represented the archetype of love and beauty, then the irony of Baartmann's nickname is obvious. Baartmann was not a goddess—she was grotesque and inspired revulsion and possibly lust but nothing close to love or beauty. She may have also been a rebuke to white Frenchmen and the frequent sexual relations they had enjoyed in the colonies (which would no longer be accepted in the metropole). She thus represented the antithesis of Frenchness—inappropriate sexuality, feminine aggressiveness, and excess. Emphasizing these differences revealed the menacing power of all females of all races and thereby reinforced the need to dominate them.

Baartmann's body and her image were used to establish nationalistic boundaries, with her supposed abnormalities exaggerated to articulate what was considered excessive in French society, a lesson that needed to be conveyed to returning émigrés and newly arrived colonial refugees. The production of Baartmann as a type both satisfied France's need to remember a different version of the Antillean colonial narrative and established and regulated normative French behaviors at home.

THE HOTTENTOT SPEAKS,
OR DOES SHE?

Not only was Baartmann exhibited in Paris as a human oddity, but her voice was fictionalized as a way of discussing a series of compelling issues before the French public. In this way, her body and her voice functioned as a representation of celebrity and brought in currency for her owner and the satirists and other writers who appropriated her. One of the most notable efforts to manipulate Baartmann's identity flowed from the pen of Charles-Joseph Auguste Colnet du Ravel (1768–1832), a royalist and former exile, journalist, poet, bookseller, and renowned satirist. His works provide a compelling illustration of racial ventriloquism from white Frenchmen using the black female body.

As a royalist, Colnet was likely to lean toward aristocracy and against the former Jacobin patriots. A longtime contributor to the *Journal de Paris* and the *Gazette de France* and an outspoken critic of Napoleon who was under surveillance by the Paris police, Colnet wrote a variety of commentaries on events of the day, including a series of satirical letters supposedly penned by Baartmann that appeared in the *Journal de Paris* in November 1814. In 1825, the letters were republished in a collection of Colnet's writings, *Mœurs françaises: L'Hermite du faubourg Saint-Germain*.[9]

Newspapers wielded significant cultural influence at this juncture in French society, and they frequently mentioned blacks. In 1814, for example, the highly influential *Journal de l'empire*, an anti-Napoleon publication that printed the debates and decrees of the National Assembly, mentioned blacks more than fifty times in connection with such topics as the colonies and abolition as well as the "traite des nègres" (slave trade).[10]

In casting his satirical critique from the perspective of a foreign woman, Colnet drew on a familiar French literary device that dates back at least to Montesquieu's 1721 *Lettres persanes* (Persian Letters). According to Montesquieu's fictitious Persian nobleman, "The inhabitants of Paris display an excess of curiosity which verges on the absurd. When I first arrived I was stared at as if I had been sent from heaven: old men, young men, women, children, they all wanted to see me.... Amazingly, I found portraits of me everywhere; I saw myself multiplied in all the shops, upon all the mantelpieces, so fearful were they of not having seen me enough!"[11] It is as if the man has no idea that he is the curiosity and that his racialized status both allows him access and highlights his inability to access French life. The imagined perspective of foreigners was a useful tool for the social critic, enabling the author to use naïveté and earnestness to offer a biting critique of morals and cultural values. As John Howland writes, "Putting social satire in the guise of a letter from a non-native exemplifies the posturing that is a potential part of all epistolary communication."[12] This kind of social satire provokes a specific response or reaction in accordance with the writer's existing views and invokes issues of difference. Conventional etiquette in form and content can be ignored or subjugated to the more important social, cultural, or political message at hand.

When Colnet began publishing his letters, Baartmann had already become extremely popular in Paris, and a play about her, *La Vénus hottentote; ou, Haine aux françaises*, opened at around the same time. He seized the opportunity offered by her presence to air his views, assuming her voice to speak "truths" that he believed Frenchmen and -women needed to acknowledge and obey. Baartmann simultaneously encompassed not merely Orientalism but also a racialized framework that accommodated blackness. Channeling Baartmann's perspective allowed Colnet to discuss happenings around Paris through a particular ideation of a black female body.[13] Colnet invented a version of Baartmann so that he could criticize his opponents by telling the stories of white Frenchmen and -women behaving badly. Baartmann's race as well as her gender "save" the nation from inept men such as Napoleon and reinscribe a Frenchness based on a true virile French masculinity and on unexamined but highly visible indications of whiteness.

Appearing on 7 November 1814, Colnet's first satirical letter from Baartmann to her fictional cousin and lover begins, "My friend, I am happy here as I was bored in London. The air of Paris suits amiable women. Nowhere have I elicited such a high degree of curiosity. They're coming from every which way to see Sartjée. These people are not disgusted!"[14] Colnet was correct that Baartmann aroused curiosity, though it is unlikely that she found her time in London, which included significant legal wrangling, boring. Colnet's reference to the lack of French disgust constitutes both a nod to that British court case and a foreshadowing of the simultaneous fascination and disgust that she engendered in Paris. Readers would have understood the irony in "Baartmann's" seeming lack of awareness of the reactions she provoked.

Colnet compares contemporary white Frenchwomen with their imagined Hottentot counterparts, as "Baartmann" declares, "some women of high birth do not express themselves with greater elegance than the Hottentot Venus." "Baartmann" enjoys her conversations with Frenchwomen, who "speak little" but tell her their most "important secrets," a phenomenon she attributes to her "foreignness." Nevertheless, she is "not easily fooled" by what she observes.[15]

The letter goes on to recount "Baartmann's" life in Paris, detailing her interactions with French people and their reactions to her. Colnet ironically pokes at imperial fashion by having "Baartmann" write, "Other than the Hottentots, Frenchwomen are the most beautiful women on earth, but out of modesty, they do not want anyone to know it. Their manner of dressing hides what is most enjoyable about them."[16] During the Napoleonic era, aristocratic Frenchwomen favored cleavage-revealing dresses that bourgeois society generally considered obscene. The irony works on two levels. First, the implicitly ugly Baartmann compares her beauty favorably to that of Frenchwomen—Colnet's feelings about the ugliness of Baartmann's actual visage are clear here; he finds her disgusting. Second, the real Baartmann was displayed in attire considered immodest, yet fashionable "civilized" Frenchwomen also wore revealing attire.

"Baartmann's" account depicts Frenchwomen as foolish, stupid, shrewd, and cunning. After a season during which Frenchwomen dressed in a Chinese manner, she tells her new French friends to adopt Hottentot fashion. Here, Colnet's satire accuses Frenchwomen of failing to show national loyalty and love of country at a time when their male counterparts are fighting a war for France's future as a major European power. Instead of contributing to this effort, the women are engaged in an inexplicable "war of hats." Whereas Frenchwomen wear theirs so high that one "must stand on tiptoe" to touch the top, Englishwomen wear theirs so low that they can barely see. According to "Baartmann," "Thus it came down to who [English- or Frenchwomen] would, out of national pride, make themselves the ugliest; and for a while it was feared that this war of hats might become the cause of a more serious war between the two peoples." Finally, contrary to the actual Baartmann's forced exhibition, Colnet's Baartmann writes of being "invited" to dances, allowing him to juxtapose Hottentot dancing, which he believes mimics animals and exposes genitalia, with passionless and unpleasant French dancing. Here again, Colnet mocks Baartmann's supposed ignorance about her own manner of behavior.[17]

The second part of the letter concerns a sex scandal that involves an angry husband whose effort to shame his wife backfires. The account is likely based on contemporary gossip about an actual couple, and readers probably knew the identities of people involved, though that information has been lost. According to Colnet, the man's lack of virility and masculinity had led his wife astray, and his impotent actions prevented him from finding another woman. In "Baartmann's" words, "since his condemnation, the dismissed husband hardly dares to show his face in public, and for good reason: women would tear his eyes out to avenge the honor of their sex." In the future, he should show more confidence and less jealousy.[18]

Colnet thus defines the standard for Frenchmen, laying blame for the affair not with the adulterous wife or her duplicitous lover but with the whiny and incompetent husband. Husbands who lacked the virility to prevent others from insulting them and taking their property risked the loss of their wives. Frenchwomen needed to keep men in line, underscoring the problem that men were not policing themselves.

On 19 November 1814, the *Journal de Paris* printed "Baartmann's" second letter, which blames Napoleon for France's recent military defeat. Unlike the first letter, this one does not mention women at all but instead focuses on men, the war, the role of journalists, and the failures of the French nation. Though "people have said . . . too many bad things about the French," "Baartmann" calls on Frenchmen to rally on behalf of the national cause.[19]

The letter begins by shoring up the image of a chivalric French military manhood. France might have real problems, "Baartmann" wrote, but at least it was populated by honorable "warriors," not "idle" ones like the Hottentots. Here, then, African inefficacy is the foil for French masculinity. If these French warriors, fearless to the point of recklessness, have a fault, it is that they sometimes worry fanatically about rising in rank. As a result, they so flaunt their bravery that those who come home unwounded or even alive feel ashamed for having let down their country:

> They accuse cannonballs of having done them a favor; they reproach the bombs for having missed them on purpose in order to interfere with their professional advancement. . . . They complain less of an arm they have lost than of the one they have left, and they hope to get rid of it at the first opportunity. In the meantime, they want at least one ostensible decoration, a fair and honorable recompense for their bravery, and attest to all that, if they are still alive, it is not their fault, and that they were well-enough behaved to deserve to die.[20]

Zealous does not even begin to describe these men. On the one hand, they care about defending France; on the other hand, lust for personal advancement colors their judgment.

Such men surely should emerge victorious; therefore, according to Colnet, Napoleon bears responsibility for their defeat and the loss of the "most beautiful of empires": "The head of these brave men, the man whom their courage and good fortune elevated to the highest point of glory and power," saw his role with "more philosophy." He lost "the most beautiful empire in the world, and he bore it wonderfully. The importance that he gave to life, in such circumstances, has astonished many people so accustomed to scorning death."[21] The ousted Napoleon becomes an easy scapegoat for a myriad of military and thus imperial failures.

Colnet's wrath also extended to "another species of brave men: warrior-speechmakers (geurriers-discoureurs)." It is not clear whether Colnet is referring to specific people, but he opines that even obsessed field soldiers are a cut above vulturish speechmakers who do nothing but talk, pretending to know everything but in actuality spreading lies and claiming secret knowledge. Peace brought them no happiness; rather, they continued to hope for global chaos so that they would have something to do. Legends in their own minds, they asked for money and medals to prove their worth and sought to be called soldiers. Despite writing of battles that never took place, spreading false rumors of soldiers' deaths, and engaging in other demoralizing behavior, these men had the audacity to "believe the honor of France is compromised if they have nothing more to say and no battles to describe."[22] Colnet's indignation at Napoleon's propaganda machine juxtaposes these supporters with exiles writing against Napoleon.[23] Colnet likely is attacking the new Chambers established by the charter of 4 June 1814: as a royalist, he would have been suspicious of legislative bodies. "Baartmann's" letter renders illegitimate both these speechmakers and their leader.

The letter continues by noting that even if the French sometimes "forget their natural lightheartedness" and are prone to melancholy, "they are lively, irascible, but their rancor does not last long and their vengeance is not cruel" with the exception of "certain individuals who had abused the privilege that powerful men have to oppress and harm others." Napoleon and his followers "have been let off with shame, quite a mild punishment for those who for such a long time had advantageously abandoned their honor." Colnet's Baartmann ends by praising the French for their compassion toward Napoleon: "This trait alone would suffice to acquaint you with a nation about which many good things could be said if one set out to depict its good qualities rather than its poor ones."[24]

The highly gendered subject matter of the two letters illustrates Colnet's rather misogynist critique: French masculinity is at risk because the women are fighting over tall hats and refusing cultural directives to stay in the private sphere where they belong. Men's actual warfare and subsequent defeat are displaced onto misbehaving women. Colnet uses Baartmann's position outside French society to highlight his compatriots' folly and to call for the regulation of white Frenchwomen. As Lennard J. Davis observes, "The emphasis on nation and national fitness obviously plays into the metaphor of the body. If individual citizens are not fit, if they do not fit into the nation, then the national body will not be fit."[25] By placing his challenges in the mouth of a black woman, Colnet sought to make his critique sting more deeply: if even she could see such unfitness, the shame must be profound indeed.

LA VÉNUS HOTTENTOTE;
OU, HAINE AUX FRANÇAISES

Baartmann was also the subject of a popular play, *La Vénus hottentote; ou, Haine aux françaises* (The Hottentot Venus; or, Hatred of Frenchwomen), although it does not name her explicitly. Written and composed by Marie-Emmanuel-Guillaume-Marguerite Théaulon de Lambert, Nicolas Brazier, and Armand d'Artois, the production premiered at the Théâtre du Vaudeville on 19 November 1814 (the same day that Colnet's second letter was published).[26] It is not clear whether the authors intended to capitalize on Colnet's ventriloquism or were merely using something already in the popular imagination, but the timing is probably not a coincidence.

Baartmann is not really a character in the play; rather, the plot places one of the characters, Amélie, in "Hottentot" costume. One reviewer noted that "before seeing the copy, I had wanted to see the original: for comparison, it is necessary to know the two points of comparison." He was sorely disappointed to discover that the play featured "a skinny, slender Venus, vivacious like the loves of which she is said to be the mother. . . . Mademoiselle Sartjée alone was worth at least two Riviera girls."[27] (Mademoiselle Rivière played Amélie in the production.) This description and the fact that the reviewer did not comment on the actress's race indicates that she was white. A reviewer in the *Gazette de France* wrote that "the contrast between the pretty figure of this actress and that of the little monster who should really stop being exhibited in public led to a nice surprise"—again denying Baartmann's humanity.[28] Although she is being exhibited across Paris, her appearance (unlike that of the actress) is shocking and monstrous.

The comedy's twice-divorced protagonist, Adolphe, has renounced future liaisons with Frenchwomen, whom he proclaims dangerous and distasteful after his wives have been unfaithful.[29] Although his aunt, La Baronne (the Baroness), arranges for Adolphe to marry Amélie, his cousin, he declares that he will only marry a woman from an uncivilized race, a savage who is "foreign to our customs and morals." Believing that Adolphe's desire to wed a savage is a sign of madness, Amélie and her aunt plot to bring him back to his senses, calculating that "we must deceive him in order to make him happy." Amélie pretends to be the Hottentot Venus to woo Adolphe. Although Adolphe is struck by her uncivilized behavior, he is also overcome by her beauty and decides to marry this perplexing and innocent (not French) creature. However, when the family members see a picture of the actual Hottentot Venus, they "cry out in fright" and decide that "with such a face / She cannot be a Venus." She cannot possibly be one of the Hottentots, "the people whose women are the most famous for their beauty."[30]

As with Colnet, the idea that Hottentot women are beautiful is used as a comedic device, since no white Frenchman in his right mind would find her so. When Amélie reveals herself, Adolphe decides that he will marry her even though she is the third Frenchwoman who has deceived him. The family is greatly relieved to have prevented a national and racial calamity, and everyone lives happily ever after, with each character proclaiming, "Do not abandon France."[31]

Like Colnet's first letter, the play provides substantial information regarding anxieties about proper roles for men and women and both unsettles and reaffirms gender categories. First, Adolphe again invokes the idea of the weak Frenchman, with his multiple failures with Frenchwomen indicative as much of his masculine insufficiencies as of his ex-wives' infidelities. When La Baronne tells Amélie that Adolphe is determined to marry someone foreign, Amélie exclaims, "He doesn't have any nationalist spirit!"[32] He rejects Amélie (France) for the Hottentot Venus (Africa). The play suggests that the lack of "nationalist spirit" can result in national-level catastrophe, such as the loss of Saint-Domingue. In addition, Amélie is safeguarding racial and class boundaries in the face of the danger posed by Adolphe's self-centeredness (or desire for miscegenation). Only someone pathetic (or colonial) would even think about marrying a non-French or nonwhite woman, and his most pathetic characteristic is his fleeting desire for blackness. But when he sees the truth, he realizes how blackness has deceived him.

Adolphe's narrow escape with his sanity and his masculinity intact reminds viewers of the dangers of succumbing to black libidinous female charms (the image promulgated in both France and Saint-Domingue at the end of the ancien régime) and of being weak in the face of such bestiality. Thus, Amélie tricks Adolphe for the benefit of France. Adolphe's national identity is at stake.

As in Colnet's letters, the play's rhetoric regarding the ineffectual Frenchman simultaneously builds off particular representations of white Frenchwomen as shrewd and manipulative and racializes tropes of Frenchness. For example, while the play revolves around Adolphe's acceptance of Amélie and thus Frenchness, he only comes to this acceptance through Amélie's transgression—that is, her adoption of a racialized and sexualized persona that attracts him. Amélie must assume a black racial identity to solidify France's white identity. Adolphe's attraction to the Hottentot Venus stems not only from her supposed sweetness but also from what he perceives as his ability to train her in a way that was not possible with Frenchwomen:

> I am going to finally, according to my whims,
> Have a young student
> Who knows yet nothing. . . .
> It is so rare that a husband
> Finds, alas, in this country
> An educational undertaking.[33]

Frenchwomen may be beautiful and civilized, but they are less open to proper instruction and control by Frenchmen.

Of course, the audience always knows that Amélie is white and French. Her deception is necessary to show Adolphe that he is misguided both in his attractions and in his national responsibilities. Much like the cuckolded husband in Colnet's letter, if Adolphe were a real man (in control of his wife), he would not need to be deceived. Instead, a woman must step in to cover for his deficiencies, granting her a particular kind of power. This role echoes the colonial image of the black woman as seductress, with an irresistible power over the white man. After Amélie's appropriation of this power has succeeded, Adolphe resumes his proper role as patriarch, and she must return to her expected domestic role, at least publicly. In private, however, she can reincarnate herself as the exotic and wild Hottentot woman who attracted him sexually.

Such rearticulations and reminders of proper gender roles were important as a wave of colonial refugees returned from Haiti. Codes of gender and racial behaviors tolerated in France's black colonies would not be so easily accepted back in France. The play's construction of class and racial boundaries and depiction of the dangers of miscegenation reflect French culture's anxieties. While skewering the aristocracy as ignorant and instructing the bourgeoisie about proper conduct, the play also casts Baartmann as the antithesis of acceptable French elite behavior or identity, ultimately offering a potent reminder of the dangers of transgressive gender roles.

THE HOTTENTOT "SPEAKS" AGAIN

Another representation of Baartmann's voice appeared on 25 January 1815 in the *Journal des dames et des modes*, which printed a description of a private exhibition and conversation supposedly from her point of view.[34] Here, having Baartmann "speak" her own story lends credence to her tale, but the narrative contradicts the reality that Baartmann was given or sold to her master's brother and involuntarily brought to Europe. Instead, the account focuses on the event's host and hostess and white French guests, Baartmann's male keeper/master, and the unknown man who wrote the passage. In contrast to the depictions by Colnet and in the play, this account at first appears to attempt to portray Baartmann's plight honestly and elicit sympathy for her by asking readers to substitute white Frenchwomen in Baartmann's place. However, this piece in fact represents another cultural exhibition and consumption of her: a reinscription of superior white French female beauty and male civilization.

The author reports that as he "dined a little time ago in a charming house where the master and mistress are polite and generous to an excess," the Hottentot Venus was suddenly announced and brought before the gathering. The sight terrified the white Frenchwomen present, and they ran and hid, causing the Hottentot Venus to become depressed and begin to cry. "Baartmann" then asks, "Where have you brought me, and what is my job?" The sentence suggests that she is by now used to such private presentations and is startled by the women's reaction. It also assumes that she has the autonomy to question her situation. According to the author, "Baartmann's" handler(s) force her to behave properly, and "soon enough, the reassured and curious ladies approached the African, touching her hands, her necklaces, her clothes." The writer seems less concerned with her being treated like a fearful wild animal than with her garb. Calling her "a Vénus callipige," he remarks, "In all, this is not a tempting Venus, especially when one has seen the Medici Venus."[35] The Callipygian Venus—so-called after the Greek for "beautiful buttocks"—is a statue that represents Venus with bare buttocks, looking back over her right shoulder, perhaps to admire them. The author evidently prefers the more modest Medici Venus, an example of the Praxitelian type known as *Venus pudica* or "modest Venus," who is represented as hiding her nudity. His irony further calls attention to "Baartmann's" "thighs prodigiously bouncing and protruding." The contrast between white beauty and black repugnance is articulated through the comparison of the bare buttocks of "Baartmann" and the statue, with white beauty prevailing. The Hottentot Venus is clearly to be viewed as a degraded Venus.

With "Baartmann's" melancholy abated, the members of the crowd ask her to choose the prettiest lady in the room. The fascination with beauty and whether there is a distinctive African beauty versus a French or white beauty is a long-running trope. After much debate, she chooses a woman in a red dress. When asked to find the "most tender man," she selects the author. This distinction may have been intended to admonish white Frenchwomen for being "pretty" but not "kind," and it certainly indicts them for lacking proper womanly attributes. Deciding to learn more about her and her story, the author follows "Baartmann" into her carriage, where he engages in conversation with her.[36] However, the actual Baartmann was always under the control of her masters and would never have left the party alone.

"Baartmann" then enters into confessional mode in French, English, Dutch, and Hottentot. The author apologizes in advance for his failure to make her words as "naïve" as the original conversation.[37] This literary device implies that the writer is fluent in all these languages, which seems unlikely, and that Baartmann is not very adept in any European language. Couched as a translation, Baartmann's story takes on an air of authenticity, since the author is merely recording what he is told without embellishment or alteration.

Baartmann tells an incredible tale of woe, differentiating Frenchness from blackness. Although the historical Baartmann lived among whites in urban South Africa, this fictive account locates her in a precivilized space at the time of her capture. In this version, whites snatched her from the shores of South Africa (contradicting the story of voluntary servitude she had told in England) just before she was to marry, killing her family in the process. Her only memento from her homeland is the necklace she currently wears, a gift from her fiancé. The author then departed, "really touched by her pain, not seeing a remedy."[38]

The tale then turns to an imagined story of white slavery, as the writer pictures "a young French woman, born in the rue du Mont-Blanc, or in the faubourg Saint-Germain, taking a walk along the beach in the South of France (dans le midi, sur les bords de la mer)," where she is stolen and taken to an "African port" by some Muslim pirates (barbaresques). From there, she passes through the hands of Arabs and is presented to the "savages" as the Paris Venus. "She cries, trembles, calls in vain for her dear country. She will surely die far from the sweet objects of her affections. . . . This, then, is the fate of the Hottentot Venus!"[39]

Though he apparently is seeking to evoke sympathy for Baartmann's situation in Paris, the stories he tells are neither similar to each other nor even close to her reality. First, "Baartmann" is highlighting that she does not want to be in France and does not belong there. The idea that blacks did not belong in France had already become a topic of conversation, meaning that her conclusions conveniently match prevailing sentiment. Second, when she leaves the party's aristocratic space, she discusses the uncivilized and barbaric nature of the upper classes. Thus, this piece also constitutes an indictment of the aristocracy, another concept that had already begun to appear among the

French middle classes. Third, ending the story with the French Venus removes France from the horrors of Baartmann's capture and kidnapping. This anecdote may have been intended to remind white readers of the negative effects of enslavement but ultimately misses the mark. The author's juxtaposition of the enslavement of generic white womanhood with that of a particular black woman effectively erases Baartmann's narrative, replacing it with a rather inexplicable story that exists mostly in the white European imagination.

Finally, the French Venus's capture reiterates and conflates the savagery of both Arabs and Africans, reminding readers of the tales of barbarism that were widespread at the end of the Haitian Revolution.[40] The publication was targeted at white women, but it is not clear precisely how the story is supposed to appeal to them or whether the author intended to indict Baartmann's status on French soil. Nevertheless, the account again hides whiteness and maleness behind the figure of a black woman, uplifting the former at the expense of the latter.

VISUAL REPRESENTATIONS

The construction and representation of the Hottentot Venus had the capacity to tantalize, outrage, or entice viewers—sometimes all at once. The image of her body functioned as a marker so grotesque that the viewer's gaze would naturally fall upon her and then be repulsed. Contradictions between the historical Baartmann and her portraits abound. For example, although she was only four feet, six inches tall (about seven inches shorter than the average French person of the time), she was often represented as towering over both the Frenchmen and -women standing beside her.[41] Further, naturalist Georges Cuvier's molds of her body demonstrate that painters deliberately exaggerated and distorted her features. Despite or perhaps because of their inaccuracy, these cartoons and prints serve as a useful mirror of French culture.

Louis François Charon and Aaron Martinet's *Les Curieux en extase; ou, Les Cordons des souliers* (The Curious in Ecstasy; or, The Shoelaces; 1814; fig. 13) depicts Baartmann, standing in the attitude of the Callipygian Venus, labeled "La Belle Hottentote," and naked except for a loincloth as she is inspected by two Scots soldiers (who represent the military occupation of a humiliated France in the wake of the Battle of Waterloo). In this image, Baartmann serves merely as a surrogate for satirizing the British in France and white Frenchwomen's behaviors. The image also highlights what the introduction of "foreign" elements can do to a "civilized" society: all of the whites shown are behaving in direct opposition to French civilized behavior. Because Baartmann is marked as uncivilized, her presence, however submissive, evokes uncivilized behavior. For example, the first man has his leg on a chair, thereby enabling the white woman to see under his kilt. Although his erection is not visible, his sword hangs between his legs, drawing the viewers' eyes to that spot. While reaching for Baartmann's buttocks, he utters, "Oh! godem quel rosbif!" (Damn! What a roast beef!). (*Roast beef* is a French insult for an Englishman so the slight is twofold: slander of the British and a salacious insult to Baartmann.) The second man gazes at Baartmann's genitalia and exclaims, "Ah! que la nature est drôle!" (Ah! isn't nature amusing!). A Frenchman looks through his monocle and remarks, "Quelle étrange beauté!" (What strange beauty!). The white Frenchwoman ties her shoelaces, looking through Baartmann's legs to see under the Scotsman's kilt, a sight that causes her to declare, "À quelque chose malheur est bon" (From something bad [i.e., her untied shoelace] a good thing happens). Even a dog is similarly affected, sniffing under the second man's too-short kilt.[42]

Baartmann is depicted like a slave on an auction block. She is passive, with no control over the circumstances, and makes no attempt to cover herself or her outsized buttocks; rather, her hand is raised as if beckoning further scrutiny. Because only Baartmann's labia are covered, the viewers' eyes are drawn to the area as they imagine—without retri-

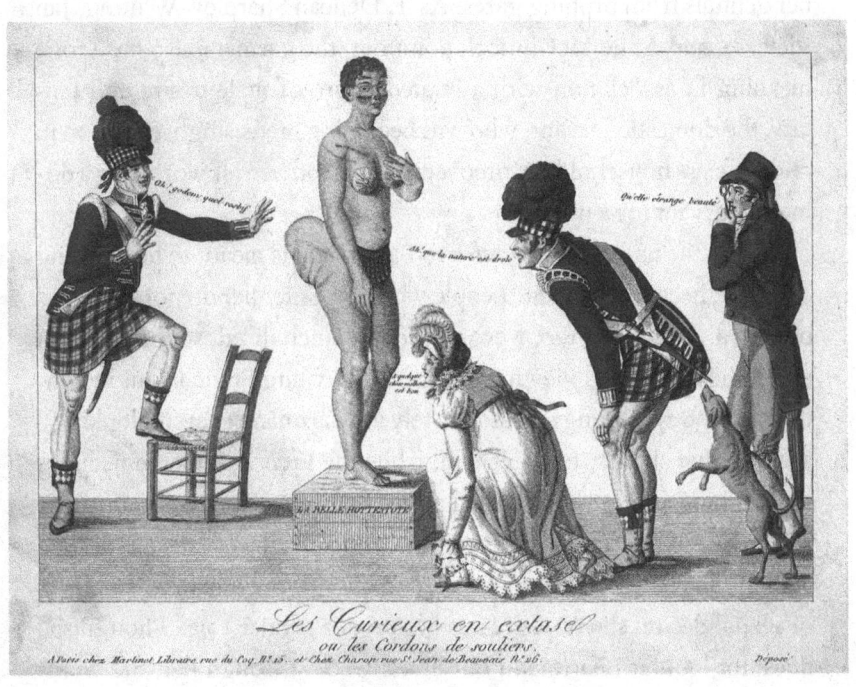

FIGURE 13.

Louis François Charon (1783–1831) and Aaron Martinet (1762–1841),
Les Curieux en extase; ou, Les Cordons des souliers, 1814. This satiric image uses Baartmann's
likeness to represent how civilized society could be easily tainted by foreign influence.
Reproduced with permission from the British Museum, London.

bution—what mysterious, dangerous, and delectable object might be hidden. As Jill Fields notes, "The core of Hottentot eroticism was the much-discussed apron, the extended labia minora." Of course, *apron* is more commonly used to refer to an article of clothing, and caricatures of Baartmann frequently depict her wearing a small apron to shield her genitals from probing gazes. As T. Denean Sharpley-Whiting, Jan Pieterse, and Anne McClintock point out, the garment also has erotic meaning in association with a related figure of male desire and fantasy, the domestic servant, who was becoming increasingly common in middle-class households. Moreover, Baartmann herself worked as a domestic servant for a time.[43]

Again, the use of *belle* to refer to Baartmann is meant to be amusing or ironic, because the white people who encounter her do not see her as beautiful. The Scots, too, were considered uncivilized, so the image in effect shows savages viewing savages. The white Frenchman, in contrast, is merely looking dispassionately at Baartmann (yet still looking), a stance that slightly elevates him, while the Frenchwoman objectifies the foreigners and thus extracts a modicum of revenge. In addition, the reference to shoelaces in the print's subtitle privileges her perspective among the characters represented, and by viewing a man as an object of sexual desire, she transgresses her proper gender role. Though she does not look at Baartmann but literally sees through her, the woman's overt sexual gaze constitutes yet another example of the corrupting effects that Baartmann's mere presence has on both white men and women: as Clifton C. Crais and Pamela Scully point out, "White women, even the most civilized, were liable to fall victim to their animal instincts and passions, to revert to their Hottentot selves."[44] The humiliation of occupation can be seen as a reminder of the humiliation suffered by French refugees who hid under beds during the fighting in Haiti instead of aiding women under attack or of those in the metropole unwilling or unable to discern proper modes of behavior.[45]

That the woman's actions are unnoticed by the men is beside the point—the audience certainly sees what she is doing. In fact, the men in the image are unaware precisely because their gazes are directed away from civilized (white) beauty by the unnatural spell cast by the hypersexual Baartmann. She thus posed a danger to white women by diverting white men's attentions and threatened white men because they lost control around her. The work pointed viewers to issues of potential miscegenation while reinforcing fears about corruption caused by the existence of blackness in both the colonies and the metropole. The scene illuminates sexual primacy's ability to make racial boundaries and thus racial hierarchies permeable.

Another image, Aaron Martinet's *Le Prétexte* (The Pretext, 1815; fig. 14) also shows curious Parisian women trying to figure out what Scottish soldiers wear beneath their kilts. Again, elite Frenchwomen are depicted as led to behave inappropriately as a consequence of foreign encounters. France had been humiliated not only by military defeat but also by occupation by savage foreign soldiers and by the fact that they were receiving the attention of civilized Frenchwomen. By showing Frenchwomen ridiculing the soldiers, however, Martinet made them seem less intimidating. But they are still looking at men that are not French.

The right side of this image, however, shows a white Creole woman (she has darker skin than the Frenchwomen and wears a head covering) selling food to the soldiers. Whereas the "proper" white ladies are overtly breaking sexual taboos, however, the lower-class woman appears to behave appropriately, perhaps signaling that the presence of savages poses a threat to aristocratic privilege. A class distinction clearly exists between the vendor and the peeping women, with the head wrap and darker skin serving as important colonial markers. This may suggest a worrying alliance between working-class and aristocratic women, who might be trying to put revolutionary distinctions in the past, or allegiances between the two foreign elements against Frenchness. Yet the overt and taboo sexuality is most strongly associated here with aristocratic women, possibly part of the middle-class delegitimization of aristocratic freedoms.

FIGURE 14.

Aaron Martinet (1762–1841), *Le Prétexte*, 1815.
The behaviors of the French female subjects in this depiction emphasize
the innate threat posed by foreign influence on French society.
Photo by Hulton Archive/Getty Images; reproduced with
permission from the British Museum, London.

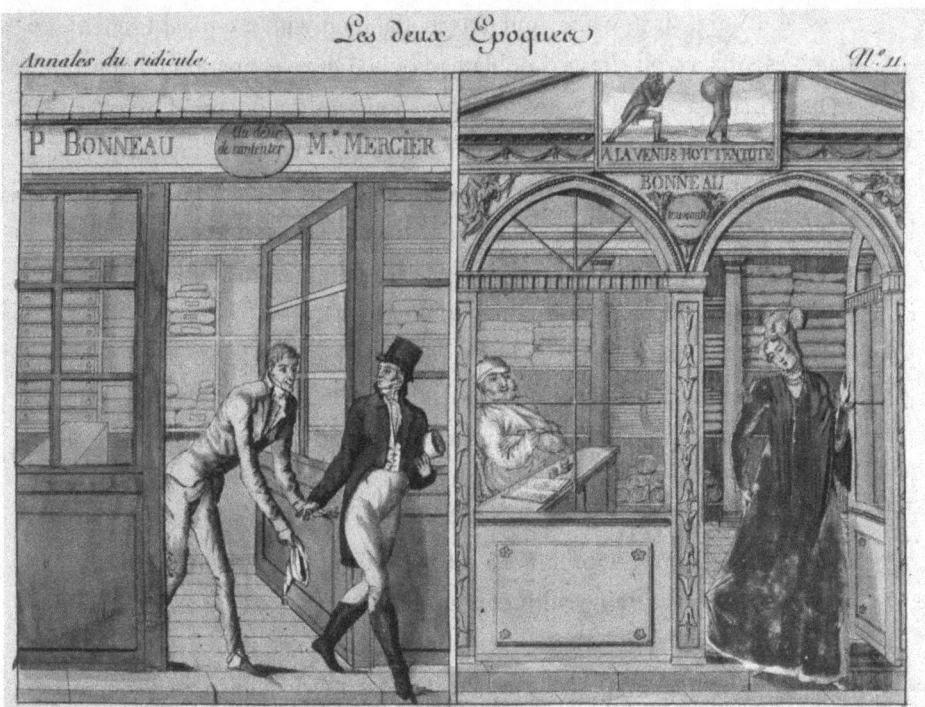

FIGURE 15.

Anonymous, *Les Deux Époques*, from *Annales du ridicule; ou, Scènes et caricatures parisiennes*, 11 April 1815. This image demonstrates the perceived negative distortion of Parisian society by foreign influence. Reproduced with permission from the Collection Grob/Kharbine-Tapabor, Paris.

Another 1815 image, *Les Deux Époques* (The Two Epochs; fig. 15) presents what the anonymous artist perceived as a rather disturbing trend: the deterioration of Parisian standards at the hands of a foreigner. The first scene shows a proprietor in the early years of his business. A young, slim, white, and deferential man with a typical French name escorts a well-dressed nobleman out of the elegant shop, happy to have made a sale. The second scene shows a shop operated by a fat and unhelpful man with a "Middle Eastern"–sounding name, *Ali*; an unescorted lady is leaving the establishment. The artist thus presents white Frenchmen as understanding and purchasing homespun fabrics while white Frenchwomen have a taste for imported and luxurious fabrics.

The shop's name uses the feminine *Bonne* although Ali is a man, perhaps to indicate that he is less than masculine. In addition, tacked prominently above the nameplate is a poster advertising the appearance of the Hottentot Venus, though only her buttocks—the most important part of her hypersexuality—are visible. Not only does her presence heighten the foreignness of the setting, but her racial difference and her positioning with commodities that are easily and sometimes problematically purchased underlines the idea that all three of the figures in the second scene are ineligible to participate in the French body politic.

CONCLUSION

Sarah Baartmann served as a foil, establishing and regulating normative French behaviors to reverse what was seen as the degeneration of white French male virility and increasingly inappropriate behavior of white Frenchwomen and to help white Frenchmen regain a sense of control. French excesses became mapped as Other in part because the extremes of Napoleon and his failed empire had proven detrimental to France. The Hottentot Venus became a terrain for projecting so much of what was perceived as dangerous for French national identity—gender inappropriateness, class transgressions, and miscegenation. Her supposed abnormalities were exaggerated to articulate all that was excessive in French society at the same time that superiority meant consuming her as a spectacle. Napoleon emerged as the face of colonial failure, and Baartmann was showcased as a cultural distraction onto which that failure could be mapped. Moreover, the dialogue surrounding Baartmann and other black women who were not entitled to the protection or respect offered to certain white Frenchwomen allowed white women a role in the definition of the French nation and in protecting the nation from blackness. Baartmann ultimately became a teaching tool of sorts, a vehicle for promoting larger discussions about blackness, whiteness, and acceptable gender roles.

At a time when the French might have felt as if they had lost all control over their empire and imperial status, reducing powerful black bodies to harmless spectacle assuaged fears and smoothed out conflicts among segments of a fragmented society, providing a much-needed unifying force. Sarah Baartmann's representations facilitated a new collective narrative intended to secure white superiority in a historical moment of flux, change, and uncertainty.

CHAPTER THREE

OURIKA MANIA
CULTURAL CONSUMPTION OF (DIS)REMEMBERED BLACKNESS

> The first ambition of the colonized is to become
> equal to that splendid model and to resemble
> him to the point of disappearing in him.
> —ALBERT MEMMI, *The Colonizer and the Colonized*

On 22 May 1824, the *London Literary Gazette* published a front-page review of a new book that it called "a very pretty story" published about a month earlier in Paris. The novel, *Ourika*, by Claire de Durfort, Duchesse de Duras, had become quite popular in the City of Light, resulting in what the paper called "Parisian *Ourika-mania*": "Every thing in fashion, and drama, and picture, has since been Ourika. There are Ourika dresses, Ourika vaudevilles, Ourika prints.... Every mouth and every Journal has rung, and is ringing with Ourika" (see fig. 16 for an image of Ourika that reflects these fashions).[1] Similarly, another London publication, *The Literary Magnet*, reported, "At Paris, 'Ourika' is a kind of talisman, that excites both the high and low, and rich and poor. You hear of nothing but 'Ourika bonnets,' and 'Ourika dresses.' In short, all Paris is 'Ourika' mad, so great an interest has this little story excited."[2] Indeed, Duras's book also spawned Ourika-

Portrait d'Ourika

FIGURE 16.

Anonymous, *Portrait d'Ourika*, 1923. From Léonel de La Tourrasse, *Le Château du Val dans la forêt de Saint-Germain: Notice historique* (Saint-Germain-en-Laye, 1924). The inscription on the top of the frame reads, "Son regard triste et joiex implore la pitié" (Her sad and happy look implores pity). The bottom inscription is taken from Psalm 27:10: "Mon père et ma mère m'ont abandonné: mais le Seigneur a pris pitié de moi" (My father and my mother abandoned me: but the Lord took pity on me). Reproduced with permission from Bibliothèque nationale de France, Paris.

themed writings, including at least four plays, and foods such as meats and biscuits, and the craze provoked comment not only in England but also in the United States.[3]

The French, too, used *madness* and *mania* to characterize the furor surrounding Ourika, and the choice of such terms was not accidental. The usage of *mania*—a long-established medical and psychological condition—to refer to this cultural phenomenon indicates that it was perceived as more than just a harmless fad. Nineteenth-century medical professionals often used their considerable authority to label deviant behaviors *crazy* or *manic*, and this characterization demonstrates that Ourika provoked anxiety in French society. The association of *mania* with a black woman further stigmatized and diagnosed both the black female body and the desire for that body as inherently suspect, abnormal, bizarre, and wrong.[4] The desire for Ourika was considered a sickness because it raised the question of why any proper French citizen would want to culturally (and literally) consume a black woman.

Moreover, the public obsession with Ourika also involved the "manic defense" to "master and control" threatening "feelings of loss, mourning, and sadness" (as a consequence of the decline of the French Empire, national presence, and identity) that psychoanalysts associate with depression and mania.[5] The inappropriate desire for and dangers of blackness were used for private pleasure and public status by white Frenchmen and -women, some of whom even began dressing in clothing inspired by Ourika and other black characters.

White Frenchwomen and -men played at other identities by portraying black women on stage, writing as if from Ourika's perspective, and dressing as Ourika, in so doing manipulating popular (mis)conceptions of black womanhood. This type of racial drag allowed white persons to appropriate the black female identity as a means of racial uplift.

Ourika Mania coincided with the 1824 rise to power of absolutist King Charles X, whose harsh, authoritarian monarchy ultimately prompted the Revolution of 1830. Shortly after ascending to the throne, Charles prohibited slaves from leaving France's colonies, even with their masters' permission, and increased surveillance of blacks in the metropole.⁶ Ourika Mania also took place within a larger discussion about the Haitian government's payment of 150 million francs to compensate French colonials for the loss of property (including slaves) in the Haitian Revolution. When the payment occurred in 1825, the French government formally recognized Haiti's independence, bringing to an end two decades of French fantasies about regaining Saint-Domingue. Ourika Mania allowed the reappropriation of a power dynamic rooted in a pre–Haitian Revolution mentality.

During 1824, the *Journal des débats politiques et littéraires*, a widely read conservative weekly newspaper, discussed blacks forty-four times. Africa was mentioned four times, including one reference to the slave trade; Guadeloupe was discussed twice, also with a mention of the slave trade. Men of color appeared four times in conjunction with an unidentified spectacle, *Le Mulâtre* (The Mulatto). Martinique, which experienced a slave insurrection in 1822 and mass deportations two years later, was mentioned eleven times, while Saint-Domingue appeared seven times.⁷

Twelve of the *Journal*'s thirteen references to black women involved Ourika, who was the subject of several stage productions that year. As literary critic Charles Augustin Sainte-Beuve noted, "The novellas of Madame de Duras have given birth to their own little genre."⁸ According to Duras herself, "A hundred comedies have been produced about it, each one more ridiculous than the previous."⁹ Because the real Ourika was long dead, she could be consumed without any lingering feelings of guilt or hesitation. She thus constitutes an absent presence in all of these representations, a potent cultural vessel with limitless potential to be manipulated because she could not respond or refute her appropriated (and often invented) story. She differs from Sarah Baartmann and Jeanne Duval in that she was not a physical presence or threat; however, Ourika's absence provided a key component that allowed white Frenchmen and -women to bring her back to (their version of her) life for their own social and cultural gain.

THE REAL DURAS AND THE FICTIONAL OURIKA

Claire de Kersaint was born in France in 1777 to a white Creole mother from Martinique and a father who had a colonial enterprise in Saint-Domingue. She and her mother fled France after her father, a liberal deputy, was executed during the Terror. They moved first to Philadelphia and then possibly to Martinique before ending up in London, where she remained for a decade and married Amédée-Bretagne-Malo Durfort, the future Duc de Duras, whose family had owned substantial amounts of land in Saint-Domingue.[10] In 1808, Claire and her husband returned to Paris, where she lived the life of a socially prominent aristocrat, hosting an important and exclusive Restoration salon at their apartment in the Tuileries. One attendee called her one of the most adept *salonnières* in Paris, knowing how "to guide a conversation without regimenting or enslaving it." By this time, blacks were a presence in the French court, and the Duchesse de Duras would have seen them in many a stately home. In addition, the letters of the Chevalier du Boufflers (see chap. 1) were widely read and discussed in such settings, and the duchess learned about Ourika from one of these conversations in 1820 and wrote a fictionalized version of her story a few years later, with fifty copies printed privately and published anonymously in 1823. By 1824, four editions and reprints had appeared, totaling more than five thousand copies.[11]

Ourika presents the first-person story of a dying Franco-Senegalese nun. The story begins when the "Chevalier de B." purchases Ourika at a slave market in Senegal and takes her from her place of birth, an act she characterizes as having "rescued" her from slavery and placed her "under the protection of Mme de B.—it was as if my life had been twice saved." Much of the narrative details how Ourika believes herself a legitimate member of Madame's family: her "first memories are of Mme de B.'s drawing room. I spent my life there, loved by her, fondled, spoiled by all her friends, loaded with presents, praised, held up as the most clever and endearing of children." She receives "all that is considered essential for a girl's perfect education," learning to sing, to paint, to speak multiple languages, to read poetry, to dance, and to converse. Nothing is held back from Ourika, and thus nothing is beyond her reach: she receives no warning "that the color of my skin might be a disadvantage." Later, when Ourika has become a talented dancer, Madame holds a ball that the girl subsequently realizes is "really to display me, much to my advantage, in a quadrille symbolizing the four corners of the globe. I was to represent Africa." She performs with a white partner who covers his face in black crepe—"a disguise I did not need."[12] But even in the midst of these required performances, Ourika feels herself deeply cared for, and her life is filled with gentility and grace. She sees herself as French.

However, one day, Ourika overhears a hushed conversation between Mme. de B. and a friend regarding the girl's inappropriateness for marriage to a "true" (white and aristocratic) Frenchman. The marquise asks, "What kind of man would marry a negress?" and the scales fall from Ourika's eyes: "I comprehended all. I was black." In the marquise's words, one is "powerless against evils that arise from deliberately upsetting the natural order of things."[13] Ourika's previous disdain for nonaristocrats is rendered ironic as she realizes that despite her upbringing, her race precludes her from membership in the aristocracy. Moreover, by claiming that Ourika's destiny as a slave is "natural," the novel leaves slavery itself unexamined and removes France from responsibility for her enslavement.[14]

Ourika's new perspective thrusts her into an identity crisis: "My face revolted me, I no longer dared to look in a mirror. My black hands seemed like monkey's paws. I exaggerated my ugliness to myself, and this skin color of mine seemed to me like the brand of shame."[15] She grows increasingly despondent, both because of her blackness and because of the marriage of her "brother" Charles (Mme. de B.'s grandson), whom Ourika loves. When a young doctor is unable to cure her depression, she seeks solace in a dilapidated convent, where she succumbs to her illness and dies, teaching the reader that blackness is an illness as fatal to France as it is to Ourika.

Duras's novel marks the first known appearance of a black female protagonist in European literature, presenting her as a sympathetic figure during a time when blacks were rarely considered in that light.[16] Yet the novel also provides a vehicle that enables Duras to explore her anger and disappointment regarding the French and Haitian Revolutions by displacing those stinging words into the mouth of a black character. The French national sense of Otherness has become so acute that it merits an effort to imagine the subjectivity of an Othered individual. Moreover, Ourika's status as an actual black body demonstrates the extent to which French racial discourses and fantasies were predicated both on universalizing black womanhood and on real black women.

This representation of Ourika also offered a means of reminding French subjects that whiteness and Frenchness were in direct opposition to blackness. Unlike the real Ourika, who died in her late teens, Duras's fictional version survives into adulthood, enabling the author to explore a number of provocative themes, including the French Revolution and its bloody aftermath, the revolution in Saint-Domingue, and the political transitions in France in the early nineteenth century. As was the case for the use of Sarah Baartmann, whose white-imagined fictional conversations were directed at whites, having Ourika discuss things so intimately French granted Duras the ability to speak through another body deemed inappropriate to speak at all.

When the marquise tells Ourika that her love for Charles is the real reason for her melancholy, Ourika disagrees, responding that her race and social situation have brought on her unhappiness. The marquise remains unconvinced: "All your misery, all your suffering comes from just one thing: an insane and doomed passion for Charles. And if you weren't madly in love with him, you could come perfectly well to terms with being black. I wish you good day, Ourika. I'm going now. And make no mistake, with far less sympathy for you than when

I entered this room." But Ourika then confesses, "All through this, a mysterious voice cried deep in my heart: she is right." Her crisis of faith and subsequent death thus result from her inappropriate love for a white man. Ourika is both devastated by his marriage to a "suitable" woman and angered by the fact that "I was never to be a sister, a wife, a mother myself."[17] Her upbringing as a member of the French aristocracy means that her highest goal is a proper marriage and motherhood, but paradoxically, her black skin in the midst of that same aristocracy means that she can never reach that goal.[18]

Christopher L. Miller and many other writers have praised Duras's text for its progressive stance on race, but as Pratima Prasad writes, Duras constructs a "black (European) aristocrat," a fact that "tends to be lost in more generalized discussions of race."[19] In addition, although David O'Connell interprets Duras's work as advancing "the cause of abolition," I believe that she simply shores up her own precarious status as a refugee and émigré.[20] Duras and other French colonial refugees use race not only to highlight the (mis)treatment of white settlers in Haiti but also to reincorporate themselves back into French society in the metropole.[21] Duras's tale of a woman from a precarious social category refuses to acknowledge any agency for the black body while reinforcing Duras's personal homogenization process on French soil. Ourika's death in the novel can be read as the author's attempt to kill or deny her émigré identity as a means of affirming her Frenchness and constituted a precursor to the *mission civilisatrice* and the use of race to claim belonging in France.

According to Heather Brady, whether or not Claire Duras ever visited Martinique or Saint-Domingue, "her exile experience gave her direct knowledge of the plantation system and the shifting power relations in the transatlantic world." In addition, she corresponded with family members from Saint-Domingue, and she likely based *Ourika*'s "nostalgic, colonial worldview along with its condemnation of the Haitian Revolution" on the accounts she read in these letters.[22]

In *Ourika*, Duras conflates the changes of the Napoleonic era and Restoration into an amorphous conglomeration of political trauma and insecurity. According to Deborah Jenson, "This instability of historical memory in *Ourika*, in which different regimes are collapsed into one ruined historical edifice, arguably bears greater significance than a well-defined date either before or after 1804," when the novel begins. Moreover, the historical timing constitutes the only "direct allusion to this insurrection [in Saint-Domingue]—to its early phases rather than to the moment of its triumph, in 1804."[23] Duras's reluctance to see Saint-Domingue in its entirety or in a period of black power over white forces reflects her denial of the actual events there.[24]

Duras's literary erasures of the institution of slavery and of the world that existed after the French and Haitian Revolutions effectively eliminated the time of aristocratic exile and strengthened the notion of an undisturbed social order. These erasures helped to mitigate the dislocations caused by the cognitive dissonance resulting from French aristocrats' refusal to acknowledge their culpability for the loss of their colonial holdings.[25]

In Duras's text, Ourika's identity crisis coincides with the French and Haitian Revolutions and reflects Duras's views on those upheavals. Ourika refers to the execution of the King Louis XVI as "that outrage" and is relieved when Robespierre's death brings to an end the "nightmarish" Terror and the possibility that Mme. de B., too, will face the guillotine. Ourika compares the bleakness of her situation to the false promises of the republican idea: "I soon stopped being the dupe of their false notion of fraternity. Realizing that people still found time, in all this adversity, to despise me, I gave up hope." She begins to believe that even enslavement would be preferable to her current life: "Scorched by the sun, I should be laboring on someone else's land. But I would have a poor hut of my own to go to at day's end; a partner in my life, children of my own race who would call me their mother, who would kiss my face without disgust, who would rest their heads against my neck and sleep in my arms. [Instead,] here I was, condemned never to know the only feelings my heart was created for."[26]

But the Haitian Revolution has eliminated even that refuge: Ourika had "cherished the illusion that at least somewhere else in the world there were others like myself. I knew they were not happy and I supposed them noble-hearted. I was eager to know what would happen to them. But alas, I soon learned my lesson. The Santo Domingo massacres gave me cause for fresh and heartrending sadness. Till then I had regretted belonging to a race of outcasts. Now I had the shame of belonging to a race of barbarous murderers."[27] Referring to the massacres of French soldiers and settlers allowed Ourika to verbalize the barbarity of blacks in Saint-Domingue and kept that discussion within blackness so that similar atrocities committed by whites remained invisible.

For all practical purposes, Duras creates a version of Ourika who is a Frenchwoman: she receives exactly the same upbringing that Mme. de B. would have provided a white daughter. This construction went against the prevailing ideology of the time, which held that blacks were inferior to whites and could never be more than slaves. Instead, Ourika's trajectory initially suggests that blacks' progress was impaired not by their blackness but by lack of opportunity.[28] But Duras then reverses course, showing that blackness indeed places Ourika among the outcasts, trumping any other factor and meaning that she can never become truly French. Similarly, Duras's Ourika can only be fulfilled within the stable gender boundaries of marriage and motherhood.[29]

But however much Duras's narrative ultimately reinforced French conventions regarding race and gender, some readers did not greet *Ourika* with amusement or appreciation. Some contemporaries viewed the work with "suspicion": in "champion[ing] social outsiders," Duras "attacked the assumptions upon which the stratified social system of the Restoration regime was based."[30] French writer Stendahl hated the novel, as did the plantocracy in Martinique.[31] In fact, Duras endured "ridicule and notoriety," as women at other Paris salons "nicknamed her Ourika ... and her two daughters Bourgeonika and Bourika."[32] Some of this mockery may have reflected garden-variety salon pettiness and/or the criticism that frequently accrued to a woman in the public arena, but the racial dimensions of these attacks may also indicate that her critics saw her as a traitor to her aristocratic class.

Detractors chose to chastise the duchess not for usurping gender roles through her writing but by equating her with her black protagonist. This implication of colonial blood called into question her Frenchness and rendered both her and her daughters, like Ourika, unsuitable for their noble station. Further, as Marylee S. Crofts notes, because the work of women writers was seen as autobiographical and Duras's protagonist was black, the duchess herself was perceived as an inauthentic aristocrat.[33] Even though she possessed some power, it was not enough to fully protect her, and others manipulated her writing on Ourika to raise the threat of exile as punishment for Duras's supposedly sympathetic portrait of a black woman. In contrast, there is no record that the male Colnet received criticism for his appropriation of Baartmann's voice for satire. A white man could be permitted to engage in minstrel drag, but a white woman who attempted to address racism by adopting a black woman's voice brought scorn. The gendered identity of the ventriloquist was thus more important than the message conveyed.

Duras's text both rebukes civility and race and reinforces racialized attitudes and practices. Even though she was not a refugee from Saint-Domingue or a native of the colony, Duras remained tainted by her alleged colonial past and her association with blackness, and this taint provided grounds for white French society to attempt to silence her and others who shared that association. Concurrently, Duras could use Ourika's so-called piety and sacrifice as proof of her own. Or more dangerously, white Frenchwomen might assert their own sexuality by presenting white Frenchmen with an understanding of the alleged power of black female sexuality (a strong theme in French colonial rhetoric). These responses spoke to the larger tensions within French society arising from the reintegration of colonies and metropole. But whereas Duras's appropriation of Ourika's voice imperiled the duchess's social standing, the fictionalized Ourika captivated and became a model for other writers and artists as well as for other aspects of popular culture.

FASHION AND FOOD

One aspect of Ourika Mania involved clothing items, perfumes, and hairstyles. Fashion experts spoke of Ourika collars, feathers, cuffs, and ribbons, while light chocolate and shades of blue, orange, and red became known as "Ourika colors."[34] Clothing with these features was described as "à la Ourika" or "à l'Ourika."[35] *Le Diable boiteux* (The Lame Devil), "a journal of shows, manners, and literature," declared that "the sellers of fashions and new accessories have been more lucky in taking the name of the heroine to give it to the ribbons, flowers, or hats that they display in their stores." The hats were made of "pink crepe, made with knots and edgings of black satin, and even black velvet, and which have for ornamentation Scabiosa or black tulips; those are *Ourika* hats (des chapeaux à l'*Ourika*). Do you see, on the small bonnets covered in flowers, those that offer red petals with a heart or a black spot in the middle? Those are *Ourika* flowers. The red and black ribbons, or pink and black, are also *Ourika* ribbons; it is this mix of colors that forms the color of *Ourika*." Even men "dress up in the *Ourika* (se mettent à l'*Ourika*); the drap-zephir (fine wool) frockcoats, the color black as the head of a negro, including the collar but without tie, so we can button just so, the buttons are encased in fine silk, tailors call these *Ourika* coats." In addition, men wore pants in "strange and ungraceful styles," with "savage and cavalier names.... The most elegant are in white tick or linen, with satin trim; some trimmed in goathair, some with yellow straw stripes; some in merinos in clear colors; others in cashmere, but whatever fabric is used, stripes are in fashion."[36] A fascination with Ourika and other black women led members of the white bourgeoisie to clothe themselves in blackness.

A decade prior to Ourika Mania, Colnet had alleged that white Frenchwomen were susceptible to disregarding good sense in the name of style, and a character in the play about Sarah Baartmann, *La Vénus hottentote; ou, Haine aux françaises*, declares, "All our ladies have already ordered for this winter dresses and overcoats in Hottentot styles."[37] Though such "Hottentot styles" apparently were merely satirical in 1814, they became fully realized with Ourika.

If purchasing and wearing blackness through Ourika was insufficient, she could also be eaten. One critic in Germany reported hearing that "Parisians could consume Ourika cutlets and Ourika biscuits."[38]

THE OURIKA PLAYS

Duras's novel inspired several dramatic productions on both sides of the English Channel. *Ourika; ou, La Négresse* (Ourika; or, The Negress), by Ferdinand de Villeneuve and Charles Depeuty, opened on 24 March 1824 and ran until 4 April at the Théâtre du Gymnase-Dramatique, while *Ourika; ou, La Petite Négresse* (Ourika; or, The Little Negress), by Mélesville (Anne Honoré Joseph de Duveyrier) and Frédéric Adolphe Carmouche, ran from 24 March 1824 through 14 April 1824 at the Théâtre des Variétés. Eight performances of *Ourika; ou, L'Orpheline africaine* (Ourika; or, The African Orphan), by Jean-Toussaint Merle and Frédéric de Courcy, took place at the Théâtre de la Porte Saint-Martin between 3 April and 13 April.[39]

Though these plays differed from one another, the productions always featured a title character who was in love with a man with whom she had grown up, and who fell in love with someone else, and her ultimate problem always involved race. All of these works were rooted in the notion that the races must remain separate.

Ourika; ou, La Négresse takes place in Marseille rather than Paris. In this version, Ourika is adopted by her father's master, who dies and leaves her his fortune. Ourika is in love with Édouard, and she believes that he reciprocates because he asks her to address him familiarly. She wants to marry him and be his "faithful slave," which is ironic because she is already his property.[40] Édouard, however, loves Élise. Although a black seaman, Captain Jack, is in love with Ourika, she remains uninterested in him. At one point, Ourika sings a "Creole" song, although it is unclear how she knows it or why she would sing it: according to the novel, she would be much more likely to sing a French song. But such a song would not have been in keeping with audience expectations and would have made Ourika seem too French.

Black Jack urges Ourika to return with him to "our country," where she will find him less ugly.[41] Élise sees the intimacy between Ourika and Édouard and initially believes that he loves her. He is horrified at the idea, however; although she has good qualities, she is outside of society. Realizing that Édouard loves Élise, Ourika gives them her fortune, and she and Jack sail for Africa. The story appealed to white audiences with the message that France was never Ourika's true country.

Ourika; ou, La Petite négresse features the same characters as the novel but is set in the slave port of Bordeaux. "Pauvre Ourika" (Poor Ourika), as she is known throughout the play, shares the stage with Madame de Beauval (in a rather lazy attempt to keep the name sounding like Beauvau) and her Creole brother, Franville. Ourika believes herself to be the adopted child of Madame de Beauval, with which Madame concurs. To entertain Franville, Ourika sings to him, assuming a "Creole" air. The main conflict, other than the obvious issue of race, is a misunderstanding between Franville and his intended, Anaïs. His jealousy—which causes another character to refer to him ironically as "the little Othello"—threatens to tear them apart, but selfless, *pauvre* Ourika reunites them despite her broken heart. Anaïs, who will eventually give birth to a daughter, recoils in horror when Ourika attempts to embrace or touch her. After they marry, Ourika goes back to Africa.[42]

Ourika; ou, L'Orpheline africaine is set in Saint-Germain. The biggest difference from the other plays is not the message of segregation but the fact that it is delivered by a black slave, Zago. Having a slave convey the need to separate the races displaces white responsibility for segregation. Ourika is reminded of her status as neither a mistress of her own circumstances nor a slave—that is, between two opposing worlds that can never be reconciled. Zago assures her that slavery is better, but Ourika responds with the ultimate act of hopelessness and despair: suicide.

Some of the women who played the role of Ourika in these productions refused to color their faces for the role, demonstrating the limits of their willingness to impersonate a black woman. While Frenchwomen accepted easily removed clothing and jewelry à la Ourika, makeup that darkened the skin was seen as crossing a forbidden threshold. In addition, donning blackface could mean the end of an actress's career. The *London Literary Gazette* wrote that one Parisian actress "blacked her face to perform Ourika, but did not like her appearance in the glass, and refused the character."[43] *Le Diable boiteux* declared that performance would be improved if the lead actress were "to focus on darkening her skin, and to become a bit savage. For now, Ourika resembles more of a gymnastics and variety show."[44]

In addition, some critics expressed discomfort when the actresses playing Ourika adopted blackface.[45] According to *Le Corsaire*, one actress's black makeup completely overwhelmed her so that she could barely move. The *Journal de Paris* declared that the public would never see the actresses in blackface, no matter how "skillfully prepared, as anything more than a repulsive spectacle."[46] Unlike modern criticisms of blackface, these objections stemmed from the perception that "the blackening . . . erased the assets" of the actresses.[47] In short, blackness would rob them of their "natural" beauty and degrade them.

The debate over the appropriation of racial identity reflected societal concerns regarding offstage masquerading. If performers could try on different identities, what was to prevent others from doing so? If a white woman could darken her skin, could a black woman lighten hers? Or worse, simply pass herself off as white? What if the makeup were so effective that someone's true racial status became obscured? Haiti had already demonstrated what could happen when black people "masqueraded" as white by demanding self-determination and freedom. Could similar strategies blur accepted gender distinctions as well?

OTHER REPRESENTATIONS OF OURIKA

Literary representations of Ourika appeared in three poems: Delphine Gay's "Ourika élégie" (Ourika Elegy; 1824); Pierre-Ange Vieillard's "Ourika, stances élégiaques" (Ourika, Elegiac Stanzas; 1824); and Gaspard de Pons's "Ourika, l'africaine" (Ourika, the African; 1825).[48]

All of the poems followed Duras's basic premise: Ourika falls in love with her "brother" Charles, discovers her blackness, realizes that her race precludes a relationship with him, undergoes an existential crisis, and finally becomes ill and dies. All of her issues are connected to Charles. Gay's and Pons's renditions give much attention to Charles's wife, who is somewhat peripheral for Duras. In so doing, these authors allow a black woman to speak of and reinforce white womanhood in the same way that they, through their own white subjectivity, speak of a degraded black womanhood.

Gay, a popular writer who read several times at Duras's salon, positions Ourika (like Duras, to whom Gay dedicates the poem) as floundering under the realization of her difference. In her despair, she rejects Charles's attempt at proper inclusion in his life: "The ingrate! He calls me his sister!" Although Ourika believes that her heart is pure and that there is "nobility" in her suffering, she ungratefully and rudely turns her back on the possibility of French familial bliss as Charles's sister, choosing to exile herself and to die. Gay gives Anaïs a great deal of agency that she lacks in the novel. According to Ourika, Anaïs, unlike her rather clueless bridegroom, "had seen my tears and had understood them," realizing that Ourika loves Charles. Demonstrating true Christian charity, Anaïs feels pity for Ourika rather than needless jealousy: Anaïs's whiteness trumps Ourika's blackness.[49]

The poem is structured around metaphors of seeing and blindness. Ourika's ability to see her own blackness and her unsuitability for Charles sends her to the convent. Charles's blindness prevents him from seeing Ourika or her love for him. And an ability to see and understand Ourika's feelings for Charles allows Anaïs to be benevolent. Like Duras, Gay concerns herself with the dynamics of the love story while barely touching on the realities of Ourika's enslavement. The poem is equally about Anaïs's suitability as a mate for Charles. All the elements of proper French womanhood are here: Anaïs is kind, watchful, and demure; most important, she instinctively understands that Ourika's blackness eliminates her from white feminine competition.

Pons knew of Gay's poem and found it "charming," yet his interpretation of Ourika's story, as T. Denean Sharpley-Whiting notes, is steeped in the language of black female hypersexuality and rapid black degeneration.[50] In Pons's rendition, because Ourika can never have the love of Charles, her transformation into a cultured Frenchwoman is revealed as farce, mimicry. Ourika brazenly offers herself and a hundred other black women to Charles: "There, a hundred black beauties will come to lust after your choice; / It is I who will please you, as I am the most beautiful."[51] But he turns away, choosing the white Anaïs instead. His refusal both confounds and infuriates Ourika, causing her to berate him and then beseech his pardon. Like Adolphe's ultimate rejection of the Hottentot Venus, Charles's rejection of Ourika reinforces his Frenchness. As in Gay's depiction, Pons's Ourika sees Anaïs as a "rival" even though Charles is oblivious to Ourika's affection for him and she could never compete with a proper Frenchwoman. That Ourika thinks that they could be rivals confirms the ridiculousness of her claims.

However, the tenor of Pons's poem shifts as he references Africa and gestures to France's West Indian colonies. In Duras's tale, the terror in Saint-Domingue finally convinces Ourika of her innate barbarity as a black woman and solidifies her downward spiral. In focusing on Africa (Ourika's birthplace), Pons glosses over many of Saint-Domingue's problems and anxieties, displacing and distancing France from its losses there.

The preponderance of the literature cautioning men to beware of the sexual power of black women spoke to fears of the problematic nature of miscegenation in the colonies and to the need for refugees from Saint-Domingue to reassert their white womanhood, as did the interesting transference of the trappings of black femininity to white women via accessories such as the head wrap. Ourika's transformation in Pons's work removes some of the moral outrage (and believability) from the charge that black women often found themselves unwitting sexual pawns in white male hands. According to Léon-François Hoffmann, Pons "imagines Ourika in bed, tormented by desire."[52] The dominant trope held that black women were the sexual aggressors in the slave colonies, but Charles's choice of whiteness prevents Pons from having the opportunity to explain miscegenation—it, like Ourika's love, never enters Charles's thoughts. Because Charles chooses a white wife on French soil, Pons restores the balance of power so often perceived as missing in Saint-Domingue and elsewhere. Ourika's death removes her from further discussion, and Pons's new rendering of history references a somewhat idyllic Africa of "baobob trees" and "green oases," erasing the horrors and loss in Saint-Domingue and casting a colonial eye toward those oases.[53]

"Ourika, stances élégiaques," which Vieillard dedicated to Charles Nodier, a well-known librarian, royalist, and romanticist, provides an interesting middle ground. Love and slavery are so entangled in this rendition that both are lessened by the comparison. Blackness separates Ourika from the possibility of Charles's love: "Ah! The color that defiles my face / Awful symbol of shame and unhappiness." It is unclear whether Vieillard feels her worthy of love at all. She is, however, full of sadness at the loss of Charles and is melodramatically determined to end her life: "Alone, I will walk . . . to the tomb / To die . . . that is my lot." Moreover, she tells him that God is his only rival:

> Love Anaïs, your beautiful and noble spouse,
> Charles, Ourika, bade you farewell,

Will no longer be jealous of your ties . . .
And, for a rival, I will give you God.

As in Pons's rendering, Ourika reflects on African rather than French landscapes—"Sad Ourika! . . . under the burning tropics"—as if her Frenchness was so permeable that crisis could cause a distant land to impose itself on her current worldview, rendering it useless.[54]

In all of these poems, the black woman serves as a foil for the writers' concerns about their own lives—specifically, blackness and its connection to the colonies. The authors process these concerns through Ourika's body and through her cultural performance created by the white imagination. An underlying current of blackness subdued and white French womanhood asserted also permeates these poems. Moreover, once Ourika understands the meaning of her dark skin and becomes divorced from her life among the French aristocracy, her so-called African behavior comes rapidly forth—the hypersexual black woman.

Hypersexuality removes Ourika from true womanhood, which is based on chaste motherhood and heterosexual marriage. Her civilized presentation is merely a thin veneer, not inherent. But as Pons demonstrates, white men could have sex with a hundred or more black women and not only still be considered gentlemen but also demonstrate French masculinity and virility.

OURIKA AS A MARKER OF ALL AFRICANS AND AS EMPIRE COME HOME

The fascination with Ourika spread beyond Paris, with Lyon's Café de l'Europe changing its name to the Café Ourika in 1824. Both a spectacle and a reminder of the colonial project, the café promoted itself as having two "'African' beauties" among its servers. Reported the *Journal du commerce*, "A red scarf draws out the ebony of their skin; and without braving the heat of the tropics or the dangers of the desert, the shy Lyonnais finds himself in *Nigritie*. Celebrated, and complimented, our two *Africaines* need not lament the slave trade."⁵⁵

The term *shy Lyonnais* seems more than just a reference to social timidity: it is a description of one too shy to go to the colonies for sex with black women. The old chestnut the "heat of the tropics" returns, cautioning male readers that such an environment would make them more susceptible to the wiles of black women. But Café Ourika brought the colonies to France, adding safeguards against seduction. In addition, according to Robert Harms, "*Nigritie* was ... an imaginary construction of European mapmakers," a region where the French purchased slaves.⁵⁶ Café Ourika, too, constituted an imaginary construction.

At the café, the *Journal du commerce* explained, patrons would be attended to by "Ourikas": "Served by their ebony hands, sugar seems whiter and perhaps sweeter.... Hasten then, *Messieurs les amateurs*: the most exquisite products of our colonies will be offered and served to you by *les naturels du pays*."⁵⁷ The "exquisite products of our colonies"—sugar, mocha, alcohol, and the hands and bodies that served them—gained in appeal by their juxtaposition. "Les amateurs"—those who had never been to the colonies—could experience all their exquisiteness without exposing themselves to the accompanying dangers.

Café Ourika intertwined pleasure and exploitation: "While waiting for the theaters to procure us the pleasure of being moved by the difficulties of the sensitive Ourika, this personnage à la mode is being exploited in an altogether different manner.... Two charming Ourika[s], who have nothing black about them but their skin, work in concert with a male Ourika at this establishment.... By simply having a few glasses of punch in your head, it will be easy to persuade yourself you are in the New World, even though you have not left the place des Jacobins."⁵⁸ Since the reviewer sees blackness as more than skin color, what does he see as missing from the women at the café? The article's humor depends on a conceptual distinction between blackness-colonies-slavery and whiteness-France-freedom and suggests that intoxication might be needed to blur those lines. Finally, the author's reference to "a male Ourika" indicates that the trope has slipped the boundaries of gender to become simultaneously a place, a name, and a race.[59]

Ourika Mania represented a cultural transaction deeply rooted in a very material contract with power dynamics that demonstrated a bizarre impulse to make the black body pay for its status while buying what makes it that body. Everything and everyone depends on the code of white Frenchness to reestablish the narrative of racial illegitimacy. Multiple issues of race and gender became involved when representations of Ourika became increasingly sought-after among various classes and often served to teach white Frenchmen and -women about racial difference. The fictionalized Ourika's inability to maintain her Frenchness in the face of adversity reinforced the belief that in her essence, as a black female, she was merely an expression of racial mimicry.

CONCLUSION

For Duras, Ourika was a means to an end, helping to subdue the insecurities resulting from the author's colonial ties. Ourika Mania did the same for France as a whole.

Representations of Ourika achieved their power from the fact that she was flawless. Educated, erudite, and proper, she was the manifestation and personification of perfect Frenchness. Only upon further examination was her inadequacy—her racial difference—revealed. Whereas the image of Sarah Baartmann presented in *Les Curieux en extase; ou, Les Cordons des souliers* (see chap. 2) compared her to food and to nature run amok, Ourika, the young black aristocrat, was carefully contained by her manners and upbringing. Nevertheless, her presence in white society still constituted nature out of control. However different the two women were, they essentially constituted two sides of the same coin—both were inauthentic Frenchwomen by virtue of their race. The fictional Ourikas thus had to either leave France or die: their continued existence in the metropole meant uncontained blackness, the consequences of which included such violations of the tenets of authentic Frenchness as interracial marriage and miscegenation. Moreover, the Ourikas had to choose to remove themselves so that their departures were not the fault of France.

While Ourika mimicked white French aristocratic society, however unsuccessfully, white Frenchmen and -women problematically copied Ourika as well. As Homi Bhabha writes, colonial mimicry is

> *a subject of a difference that is almost the same, but not quite.* Which is to say that the discourse of mimicry is constructed around an *ambivalence*; in order to be effective, mimicry must continuously produce its slippage, its excess, its difference. . . . Mimicry emerges as the representation of a difference that is itself a process of disavowal. Mimicry is, thus, the sign of a double articulation; a complex strategy of reform, regulation, and discipline, which "appropriates" the Other as it visualizes power. Mimicry is also the sign of the inappropriate, however, a difference or recalcitrance that coheres the dominant strategic function of colonial power, intensifies surveillance, and poses an immanent threat to both "normalized" knowledges and disciplinary powers.[60]

Representations of Ourika reveal significant underlying tensions. For this type of appropriation to achieve even tacit tolerance, one's "true" racial and gender identity must remain clear.

Baartmann remained in living memory when Ourika Mania hit, but Baartmann was so far beyond the pale that the French did not know what to do with her. Ourika, in contrast, was long dead and was thus more manageable. The spectacle of Baartmann became consumable through Ourika. She was an Ourika doll, and Ourika's existence and consumption were entirely predicated on Baartmann and her introduction and absorption into French culture. Baartmann's presence occurred during an era when France was besieged by anxiety-provoking foreignness, but Ourika's foreignness was internal and integral to her black female body, hearkening back to a time before armies of occupation, when strangeness could be contained within that body.

The French imaginary posits that black bodies exist on French soil to enable French fantasies. When black female bodies escape containment, however, they become too real and go beyond the imaginary. When white Frenchwomen donned blackface, Ourika became three-dimensional. Confronting such a person was unappealing because it meant embodying this person and her history while actively ignoring blacks' oppression under French rule.

Likewise, the myriad Ourika-inspired consumables enabled the French to cut Ourika into pieces and avoid dealing with her as a full person. Ourika Mania thus represented a violent process in which the black female body moved from spectacle to cannibalization and dis(re)memberment.

CHAPTER FOUR

JEANNE DUVAL
SITE OF MEMORY

> For me—a writer in the last quarter of the twentieth century, not much more than a hundred years after Emancipation, a writer who is black and a woman—the exercise is very different. My job becomes how to rip that veil drawn over "proceedings too terrible to relate." The exercise is also critical for any person who is black, or who belongs to any marginalized category, for, historically, we were seldom invited to participate in the discourse even when we were its topic.
>
> —TONI MORRISON, "The Site of Memory"

In the opening pages of Gustave Flaubert's 1869 novel, *A Sentimental Education: The Story of a Young Man*, the protagonist, Frédéric Moreau, sees and falls instantly in love with Mme. Arnoux. While he is admiring her, a black woman approaches with Mme. Arnoux's child. Mesmerized by the woman's "magnificent brown skin," he stops to behold her. Frédéric "imagines" that Mme. Arnoux, "this beautiful white woman," "lived in the West Indies, and has brought the black woman back with her from 'some tropical island.'" Later, while in the Jardin des Tuileries, he sees another black woman who reminds him of

FIGURE 17.

Detail from Gustave Courbet (1819–77), *L'Atelier du peintre* (1855), showing Charles Baudelaire and Jeanne Duval, with the image of Duval erased. Jeanne Duval had been painted looking at Baudelaire, who is in the bottom right position reading a book. She was erased at Baudelaire's request, presumably after another falling out with Baudelaire. Musée d'Orsay, Paris.

Mme. Arnoux's maid, and thereafter, "every time he walked through the Tuileries his heart would beat faster in his hope of meeting her."[1] Thus, Frédéric's narrative echoes earlier narratives in this book, in which the blurring of blackness elevates and explains whiteness and appropriate sexual attraction. His memories of attraction are ignited through a combined but disavowed association of black womanhood with his fantasies about a potentially Creole white woman. Jeanne Duval, the subject of this chapter, represents the commingling of the Caribbean and France, Frenchness and blackness.

This chapter examines three sets of cultural productions of Jeanne Duval, the common-law wife of writer and poet Charles Baudelaire: those by Baudelaire himself, those by his contemporaries after his death, and those by Baudelaire's biographers. These representations present a contradictory picture of Duval: she is both angry and strong-willed and fragile; fat and thin; dark and light; frizzy- and smooth-haired; stupid and shrewish; angelic and devilish; a muse, a wife, a whore, and a lesbian; a second-rate actress and a sexual vampire of such biblical proportions that she sucked everything of value from Baudelaire and reduced him to a carcass. As Marc-A. Christophe asks, was Duval Baudelaire's Venus or his demon?[2] Yet much of the work about Baudelaire's *Les Fleurs du mal* (including the Black Venus cycle, which was inspired by Duval) has generally relegated Duval to a peripheral role, while others devote more attention to her but nevertheless interpret her life solely through Baudelaire.[3]

The narrative here, however, focuses on Duval herself, making Baudelaire simply one voice—albeit an important one—among others. Most of the firsthand descriptions of her life and of their life together come from Baudelaire's letters to his mother, Caroline Aupick, with whom he was extraordinarily close (see chap. 1). When writing to Aupick, Baudelaire frequently used exaggeration and misleadingly characterized his contemporaries, and his descriptions of Duval's alleged actions and mistreatment of him cannot be accepted as unequivocally accurate. Rather, his correspondence offers a one-sided and distorted portrait that reflects his own interests and ends, particularly his need for money. In addition, both his contemporaries and subsequent biographers have interpreted those letters in a way that fits with Baudelaire's image as an artist and poet. In short, they use information about her to construct him.

In contrast, this chapter uses him to illuminate parts of her life. Baudelaire began the cultural production of Duval, much in the same way that Colnet, Duras, and other white Frenchmen and -women mapped words and actions onto their black female subjects. But although Baudelaire's power over Duval had long-lasting impact, she outlived him and at times positioned herself to counter his characterizations, though she ultimately failed to control her own narrative.

Whereas Sarah Baartmann and Ourika were subjected to a hypervisibility, Baudelaire's contemporaries and biographers sought to annihilate Duval from his narrative. In many ways, they had great success, shaping a more insidious depiction of Duval as a means of positioning Baudelaire as a great French writer. Duval could not fit into the new imperial project that arose with the French colonization of North Africa, so his allies simply removed her after he was no longer alive to provide her with some measure of protection. New as well as unresolved colonial anxieties contributed to the need to shore up specific new kinds of Frenchness—represented by Baudelaire and other artists—and made Duval into a repository for anti-French venom. These misconceptions, in turn, contributed to Baudelaire biographers' subsequent demonization and maligning of Duval. Angela Carter and other critics who have sought to revise her characterization have, according to Victoria Tillotson, failed "to foreground the historical conditions that massively over-determined both Baudelaire's relationship with Duval and Duval's subsequent denigration. These historical conditions are the relations of capitalism and hyperbolic imperialist conquest and domination," which reached "their apex in the mid- to late nineteenth century" but began well before that era.[4] Duval thus remained fixed as a destructive black female body, solidifying the French legacy of racial ventriloquism that became so powerful with Baartmann and Ourika.

MONARCHY AND THE END OF SLAVERY

At the end of June 1830, Charles X, hoping to return to the ancien régime and faced with an increasingly restive parliament, issued restrictive ordinances that curtailed freedom of the press and legislative power. The French people responded with strikes and protests that led to the king's abdication. His successor, Louis-Philippe d'Orléans, ruled until February 1848, when a combination of economic misery and popular discontent with his repressive regime led Parisian liberals and workers to unite to overthrow the monarchy and proclaim the Second Republic. In December 1848, Louis-Napoléon Bonaparte was elected president; three years later, he joined with conservative leaders to destroy the republic from within, staging a coup against his own constitution on 2 December 1851, proclaiming himself Emperor Napoleon III, and ushering in the Second Empire (1851–70).

With the abolition of slavery in 1848, blackness became more focalized as a way to justify ongoing inequality. Baudelaire and other French subjects used Duval's representations as a medium to express their anxieties about what it meant to be French in a postslavery nation with increasing numbers of nonwhite bodies threatening the public presentation of an exclusively white country. The iconic representations of Duval perpetuated the conceptions of both black womanhood and femininity that had developed under slavery. Paradoxically, however, the intensity of the vitriol aimed at her by Baudelaire's biographers underscores her importance to Baudelaire and his work.

With the wealthy bourgeoisie having replaced the aristocracy, the debate over French national identity reopened, though the political and social changing of the guard in Paris did little to assuage the fears of middle-class white Frenchmen and -women. In the summer of 1830, at the same time that the July Revolution was occurring in France itself, the country's troops invaded Algeria, beginning the construction of a second colonial empire. France took control of the Senegalese coast in 1843 and launched colonial expeditions in Asia and Mexico in the 1860s. By the end of the century, France had not only expanded its hold on northern Africa but controlled more territory in West Africa than any other European power.

At home, unconventional bohemian lifestyles grew in popularity, attracting not only Baudelaire, Duval, and other artists but also wealthy and middle-class members of society. At the same time, the upper middle class asserted its own bourgeois identities, creating an uneasy mix. As historian Ann Stoler writes, in such an environment, "what sustained racial membership was a middle-class morality, nationalist sentiments, bourgeois sensibilities, normalized sexuality, and a carefully circumscribed 'milieu' in school and home."[5]

Duval emphatically did not fit this description and thus lacked "racial membership," which may help to explain why she so frequently experienced attacks that featured gender and racial overtones. More than just an interesting narrative about a dysfunctional relationship between two dysfunctional people, Duval's story provides insight into how white Frenchmen and -women grappled with Othered bodies during an ongoing time of social upheaval.

BAUDELAIRE'S WRITTEN AND VISUAL REPRESENTATIONS OF JEANNE DUVAL

Baudelaire's letters display a full range of emotions regarding Duval, from hate and fury to love and sentimentality. At times, he portrayed his connection to her as resulting solely from "a sense of duty," thus shifting attention away from his misbehavior and portraying himself as mature and motivated by honor.[6] At other times, Baudelaire represented Duval as deliberately trying to sabotage him and as suspicious and jealous: in 1852, for example, he told his mother, "I have to work at night in order to have quiet, and to avoid the insupportable fussing of the woman I live with." He went on to urge his mother "not to send your letters to *my house*" because "*Jeanne knows your handwriting*."[7]

Baudelaire often portrayed Duval as an impediment to more than just his creative process. In one particularly bitter 1852 letter, he declared, "Jeanne has become an obstacle not only to my happiness—that would be little enough, since I too can sacrifice my pleasures as I have proved—but also to the perfecting of my mind. These past nine months have proved a decisive experience for me. . . . *In the past she had some qualities*, but she has *lost* them; and I, I see more clearly." After criticizing her pettiness and greed, he lamented the fact that his "terrible vanity" prevented him from "leaving the woman without giving her a certain amount of money" and vowed that "since I cannot offer her a large sum, I shall continue to give her small sums of money, which will be easy, since I *gain it easily enough*, and by working hard I can gain still more. BUT I SHALL NEVER AGAIN SEE HER. Let her do what she likes." In the same letter, however, he admitted that he was "glad there are no weapons here; I think of the times when it is impossible to remain calm, and of that awful night when I cut open her head with a bracket."[8] He certainly was not blameless in their relationship.

Yet in another letter written the same year, Baudelaire confessed that despite the pain she had caused him, when faced "with a melancholy as deep as hers, my eyes fill with tears, and to tell the truth my heart is full of reproaches. Twice I've devoured her jewels and her furniture, I've made her incur debts on my behalf, sign IOUs, I've beaten her, and finally, instead of showing her how a man of stamp behaves, I've constantly given her the example of debauchery and instability. She suffers—and is silent. Isn't there cause for remorse in that? Am I not as guilty in this regard as in all the other matters?"[9]

In 1854, Baudelaire was embarrassed by Duval: "I forbade her to come and visit me here; it was my odious pride that made me do it.—I don't want people to see a woman of mine looking poor, sick, and scruffy, when they knew her as a beautiful, healthy, and elegant woman."[10] Yet two years later, he asked Aupick, "Why do you not, like all mammas, speak to me of marriage? To speak quite sincerely, the thought of that woman has never left me. . . . The poor creature is ill now and I confess it makes me sad to think she might die far away from me." He acknowledged, "For a long time she avoided me like the plague, for she knew my fearful temperament, nothing but craft and violence." But despite his constant thoughts of and sympathy for her, "I have refused to go and see her."[11] At around the same time, he also wrote, "This woman was my sole amusement, my only pleasure, my only companion, and, in spite of all inward shocks of a stormy relationship, the thought of a permanent separation had never clearly entered my mind. I've used her and abused her! I've taken pleasure in torturing her, and now I've tortured myself."[12]

In addition to the evocative descriptions of Duval that Baudelaire created with his words, a few of his drawings of her survive (figs. 18–21). The majority of the images present Duval in her younger, more vibrant years, although he did not produce at least some of them until much later, meaning that he was drawing her as he remembered her or perhaps as he wished to remember her. All of them emphasize her full bust and small waist, but her complexion is of varying shades, and her hair and features do not correspond to written descriptions of her provided by Baudelaire's friends, colleagues, and biographers. There is no way verify the accuracy of any of these accounts or depictions: Duval exists only as she has been interpreted and produced by others.

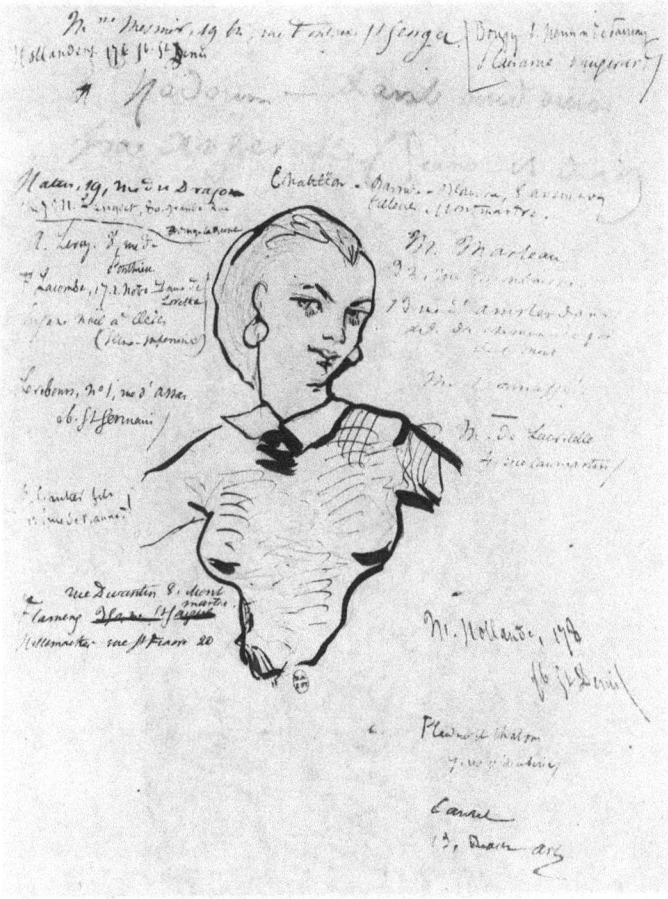

FIGURE 18.

Charles Baudelaire (1821–67), drawing of Jeanne Duval, ca. 1858–60, reproduced with permission from Bibliothèque nationale, Paris/Bridgeman Images.

FIGURE 19.

Charles Baudelaire (1821–67), drawing of Jeanne Duval, n.d., reproduced with permission from Bibliothèque littéraire Jacques Doucet, Paris/Archives Charmet/Bridgeman Images.

FIGURE 20.

Charles Baudelaire (1821–67), drawing of Jeanne Duval, February 2, 1865.

FIGURE 21.

Charles Baudelaire (1821–67), drawing of Jeanne Duval. December 31, 1849, Photo12/Ann Ronan Picture Library/Alamy Stock Photo.

JEANNE DUVAL THROUGH THE EYES OF BAUDELAIRE'S CONTEMPORARIES

In *L'Atelier du peintre* (The Artist's Studio, 1855; fig. 22), Gustave Courbet (1819–77) portrays an allegorical vision of life as a painter around 1850. The painting depicts three groups of people: ordinary Frenchmen and -women on the left, Parisian elites on the right, and the painter himself in the middle, mediating between the other two groups.[13] Baudelaire is the last figure on the right, reading a book. Courbet initially painted Duval immediately to the left of Baudelaire, squeezed between two openings, but Baudelaire asked Courbet to paint over her, and he complied, leaving only the ghost of her image.[14]

Courbet subtitled the painting *Allégorie réelle déterminant une phase de sept années de ma vie artistique et morale* (A Real Allegory Determining a Seven-Year Phase of My Artistic Life), and indeed, Duval's erasure and spectral persistence constitutes an apt metaphor not only for her life but also for what Griselda Pollock describes as "the continuing 'problem' of the presence of" black women in modern French life.[15] As white Frenchmen and -women attempted to establish a French identity, it had no place for nonwhite women such as Duval.

In 1861 Baudelaire submitted his candidacy for membership in the Académie française, prompting printmaker Emile Durandeau to produce a biting caricature that lampooned the poet's lifestyle (fig. 23). As feminist scholar Elizabeth Fallaize notes, *Les Nuits de Monsieur Baudelaire* (The Nights of Mr. Baudelaire) "depicts the poet, or rather the poet's feet, protruding from an upturned bed and surrounded by a jumble of objects associated with black magic and witchcraft, including a skeleton, a broom, a bat, a foetus in a jar, a black cat and vessels of strange shapes holding various liquids." The image would "hardly [have been] the kind of advertisement" Baudelaire would have desired as he sought to join the Académie.[16] At the head of the bed is a shadow that at first glance looks like it belongs to a cat on the floor; however, the cat has a different shadow, meaning that there is another creature

FIGURE 22.

Gustave Courbet (1819–77), *L'Atelier du peintre*, 1855. Courbet's painting depicts a symbolic relationship in which artists act as the intermediaries between the Parisienne elite class and ordinary Frenchmen and -women. Musée d'Orsay, Paris.

FIGURE 23.

Emile Durandeau (1827–80), *Les Nuits de Monsieur Baudelaire*, 1861.
This critical caricature demonstrates Durandeau's disdain for
Baudelaire's lifestyle and his association with blackness.
Artokoloro Quint Lox Limited/Alamy Stock Photo.

in bed with Baudelaire. Since his relationship with Duval was well known, the shadow may have been intended to represent her among the "black magic" objects with which Baudelaire surrounded himself?

In 1862, Édouard Manet painted Duval, a paralyzed and sickly figure he dubbed *La Maîtresse de Baudelaire allongée* (*Baudelaire's Mistress, Reclining* [also known as *Lady with a Fan*]; fig. 24). The image differs markedly from more conventional depictions that demonize Duval but nonetheless distorts the proportions of her body (her hand is nearly the size of her head) and thus creates a warped, troubled, and off-putting image of the woman.[17]

But as long as Baudelaire was alive, depictions of Duval were not uniformly negative, since he continued to care for her (see chap. 1). After his August 1867 death, however, he was no longer around to temper the vitriol directed at her. Despite the ambivalent feelings evident in his letters to his mother, she detested Duval and blamed her for Baudelaire's illness, writing, "The Black Venus tortured him in every way. Oh! If you only knew! And the amount of his money that she devoured! . . . All of these constant requests exacerbated his illness and could even have been the cause."[18]

Similarly, according to Christophe, "Baudelaire's friends were not at all enthusiastic about [Duval's] personality."[19] They had difficulty placing her within the context of his life in a palatable way, in large part because their genuine memories of the poet frequently contradicted the image of him that they wanted to present to the public. But they could reconcile these contradictions by presenting Duval as demonic or as a whore and thus as responsible for any aspects of Baudelaire's life that did not fit with that image. Moreover, her blackness and its associations became a convenient focus for this venom, and because her race precluded her from middle-class respectability, she and women like her could not fit into a new imperial France.

In memoirs written near the end of his life, Charles Toubin (1820–91), who founded a newspaper, *La Salut public*, with Baudelaire, wrote that "his mistress, as everyone knows, was a colored girl called Jeanne

FIGURE 24.

Édouard Manet (1832–83), *La Maîtresse de Baudelaire allongée*, 1862.
Manet's distorted physical depiction of Duval epitomizes the manner in which
Duval's character has been distorted over time by various friends and
biographers of Baudelaire. Szépmüvészeti Museum, Budapest.

Duval whom he caught one day in flagrante delicto with her hairdresser.... Baudelaire was furious.... 'With anyone else,' he told us, 'I wouldn't have minded, but with a barber!' Two days later, we ran into her at the Cheval-Rouge crossroads. He went straight up to her and, in front of all the passers-by, gave her a severe talking-to. He took her back a few days later."[20]

Writing in 1882, Baudelaire's longtime friend and rival, Théodore de Banville (1823–91), declared that Duval was the only woman that Baudelaire truly loved and that she "had at once something of the divine and something bestial."[21] Poet Ernest Prarond observed that "Jeanne seemed a very passive girl.... She was a mulatto—not very black, or beautiful." In contrast to Baudelaire's sketches and to other accounts, Prarond also described her as "rather flat-chested," as "quite tall," and as having an "awkward gait."[22]

The emphasis on Duval's promiscuity and the fact that she was "mulatto" and "not very black" further highlights the contradictory and dichotomous representations of her. Duval often was not portrayed as the straightforwardly monolithic savage black body so widely featured in French discourse. Bodies like Duval's had become a reality in France, and white Frenchmen and -women struggled to make sense of the confusion those bodies created.

In an 1892 proposal for a statue of Baudelaire, Edmond Lepelletier (1846–1913) used Duval to excuse Baudelaire's bohemian lifestyle, describing her as an "ugly, vulgar and wicked," negress who he claimed "prevented him from going to live in Honfleur, close to his mother.... She pursued him to all of his homes." She caused disturbances and demanded money. In Baudelaire's mind, Jeanne was "transfigured" from this "rough envelope" into "an elegant form, fine and subtle.... Baudelaire never really loved this black drunken woman. His ideal mistress, incarnated sometimes by Jeanne Duval, stood in the fog of dreams in the form of a brown, toothsome, and odorous woman from the tropics, whose inner self was as stormy as the Sea of Ceylon, and whose rough ropes, which were her braids, seemed to set sail on a voyage to the land of prolonged ecstasies and artificial pleasures."[23]

Gaspard-Félix Tournachon (1820–1910), better known as Nadar and also one of Duval's lovers, recalled that when he first met her, around 1839–40, "she was a tall girl, very tall, at least a head taller than average." The fact that she was employed was "already surprising," but in addition, "this extra-large maid is a negress, a real negress, at least a mulatress, without a doubt: tons of crushed white powder did nothing to hide the copper of her face, her neck, her hands." He found that

> the creature is beautiful for that matter, of a special beauty that didn't come from Phidias, a special stew for the refined. Under the devilish abundance of her jet-black mane her eyes—as big as soup plates—seemed even blacker; her small, delicate nose, having wings and nostrils carved with exquisite finesse; her mouth like an Egyptian, although from the Antilles—the mouth of the "Isis" of Pompeii—admirably positioned between her well-defined, strong lips. All of her was serious, proud, even a little disdainful. Her waist and torso were long, well-formed, undulating like a snake, and particularly remarkable for the exuberant, implausible development of the pectorals, and this extravagance gave the not-ungraceful impression a branch overladen with fruit. Nothing too awkward, no trace of that simian slander that has betrayed and pursued the descendants of Ham throughout the generations. Finally, her voice is friendly, finely timbred, but with unusual deeper notes.[24]

Nadar cannot decide whether he desires her, and his description simultaneously highlights her allure and constructs her as Other. In making her represent so many disparate things, he ultimately makes her represent nothing. Moreover, Nadar's emphasis on Duval as "a negress, a real negress" calls attention to and even exaggerates her blackness as a way to both exoticize and criticize her as well as to position her as bearing responsibility for many of what bourgeois morality would see as Baudelaire's faults.

The vast majority of the descriptions of Duval place her at various poles—black *or* white, skinny *or* fat, flat-chested *or* voluptuous—and in so doing create binaries that exaggerate her and ultimately make her into fantasy and erase her true character. Despite the fact that she was Baudelaire's longtime companion and as such more or less had to be accepted into French society, no one cared enough to see her beyond placing her into various discrete categories. She was dismissed as merely an appendage to Baudelaire's legacy.[25]

In the wake of Baudelaire's death, his contemporaries sought to restore him to a more elevated and respectable space in which there was no place for Duval and her blackness. At the same time, because some of his most famous poetry was based on and inspired by her, she could not be completely erased. The solution was to fall back on the tropes long associated with the black woman, most notably an exaggerated and aggressive hypersexuality. This presentation also put her in opposition to the mythical French female ideal, thereby reinforcing existing gender as well as racial boundaries. Although the representations of Duval are a product specifically of late-nineteenth-century imperialism, the basic image had changed little over the preceding half century.

JEANNE DUVAL AS A *LIEU DE MÉMOIRE*: BIOGRAPHERS OF BAUDELAIRE

As the effort to canonize Baudelaire moved from his friends to his biographers, Duval continued to pose a problem. She remained a living repository of information about him and potentially a major obstacle to efforts to shape his literary legacy to conform to (white) French norms. Baudelaire's biographers (with the relatively recent exceptions of Emmanuel Richon and Claude Pichois) consequently continued the project of evisceration and racial ventriloquism, shrugging her off as a mere nuisance, an unimportant distraction.[26] Unsure about what to do with her, these white Frenchmen distorted and subjugated representations of her nonwhite body, thus elevating and mythologizing their own Frenchness.

It is as if Baudelaire's greatness as a writer has long been predicated on her obliteration even as his most celebrated poetry depended on her existence. Of course, this dismissal of a woman of color in the life of a great white man is not unprecedented, nor is the need to manipulate black womanhood to have larger discussions about whiteness, as in the cases of Thomas Jefferson and Sally Hemings and Édouard Manet and his painting *Olympia*.[27] Venerating the man appears to require first brutally maligning or violently manipulating the Other.

This reinforcement of a male-centered narrative results in the telling of Baudelaire's story at the expense of that of his wife. Like Baudelaire's contemporaries, modern-day scholars seem to struggle to find a place for Duval in his life and often resort to the trope of the exoticized black woman.

That struggle is evidenced by the indexes to various biographies of Baudelaire. Several volumes have entries for *Duval, Jeanne* that merely direct readers to *Jeanne*.[28] Lois Boe Hyslop and Francis E. Hyslop Jr.'s edited volume of selected letters by the poet goes one step further in this erasure: there is an entry for *Jeanne* but nothing under *Duval*.[29] This denial of her name may reflect the fact that she used several different surnames, but it nevertheless contributes to the overall lack of respect for her subjectivity and echoes the pre-1848 French bureaucratic practice of denying enslaved people the dignity of a family name.

But biographers took a far more vicious approach when they did mention her. Writing in 1920, Gonzague de Reynold declared her the "vampire of [Baudelaire's] existence."[30] According to François Porché, Baudelaire's hands trembled the first time he saw "this strange apparition." In describing Duval's otherworldly hold on Baudelaire, Porché displays no curiosity about Duval's origins, motives, or perspective: "Jeanne was a native of San-Domingo. That is all we know of her origin, and even that is doubtful. But what does it matter? It is better thus. Whence she came no one knows, and after Baudelaire's death she disappears. Her beginning and her end are hidden in shadow."[31] Porché's convoluted explanation for their mutual attraction questions how someone so talented could possibly have been ensnared by a poor mixed-race specimen of mediocrity.

Porché's work continued the powerful narrative trajectory regarding Duval that Baudelaire's contemporaries had established. Tall and thin, she moved with a "kind of undulation. . . . Her head, was it ugly or beautiful? It was impossible to say; but there was about it, as about her body, something exorbitant." Her hair "fell on all sides, in spite of the hairpins, in furious wisps, like a writhing bunch of snakes." According to Porché, Baudelaire's first glimpse of Duval sent him into orgasmic expositions regarding her "shameless hips" and "writhing" hair. Only Baudelaire's "breeding" prevented him from going backstage to meet her; instead, he sent her a bouquet of flowers and left the theater "in a state bordering on agony," haunted by Duval's voice, with "its sweetly hoarse inflections, bestially caressing, and it was the contrast of the slim waist with those insolent haunches, just that, which obsessed him."[32]

Porché continues, "Stylised to-day by time, she is like one of those statues of ancient Egypt, in black marble, with enamelled eyes. At the time the sphinx lived in the rue Saint-Georges." She was also a woman in search of "a serious customer. Once she had scented good game, a well-to-do young man of family, it was for her—with her 'instinctive knowledge'—to draw him into her den."[33] Porché thus positions Duval as a stalking prostitute, a wild animal seeking her next prey.

In Porché's rendering, Baudelaire is a victim, and when he emerges from Duval's lair, he is "a little unsteady"; "invisible bonds, strong as an iron chain, already bound him to this savage Venus, who was sitting up in bed—in the daylight and whiteness of the sheets even more akin to the shadows—delicately, with the movements of a monkey, dipping her bread and butter in her chocolate." By feigning submissiveness toward her new lover, Duval acquires furniture and other trinkets as well as a more upscale address on rue de la Femme-sans-Tête, as Baudelaire "signed bills that encumbered him all his life." Using her "subtle antennae" and "her intelligence," she had begun the journey that would ruin his life, creating a situation from which Baudelaire had no escape:

> He went to see Jeanne, he was shocked as soon as he entered the room by the half-caste's vulgarity. But this sharp disgust was quickly followed by another kind of stupefaction.
>
> At these moments, however, passion was not the only power to which Baudelaire submitted, or rather, his imagination enriched this power with all kinds of spells—above all, if Jeanne were content to say nothing, if her insane chatter gave place to amorous, catlike purring, as she crouched naked before the fire. Then she would lose her personality of a third-rate actress, of a cunning, greedy prostitute, and become Beauty, impersonal and sacred, beyond all morality. . . .
>
> Confronted with Mlle. Duval, endlessly retailing her silly tittle-tattle, Baudelaire began to suffer cruelly from a degrading companionship: before this dark body, naked save for its jewels, which in the firelight threw an immense shadow on the wall, like that of the Genius of Evil stretched over the world, the poet bowed his head and worshipped.

Porché also insinuates that Duval made Baudelaire an alcoholic and was an accomplice for his "schemes" to dupe his mother out of money. When Baudelaire sent Duval with the letter discussing his suicide, his friends became alarmed. Porché proclaimed that his frantic friends found her "draped in yellow satin, lounging about with a cigarette in her mouth. From the lips of the sphinx herself [they] learnt that the poet had been carried, wounded back to his home."[34] This characterization of Duval enables Porché to avoid examining why Baudelaire was so easily manipulated by a "third-rate actress and prostitute."

Enid Starkie's 1958 biography of Baudelaire devotes an entire chapter to his "disastrous relationship with the mulatto woman, Jeanne Duval, who was to bring him so much unhappiness." Despite this negative characterization, Starkie acknowledges that Duval was the most important person in the poet's life and that "there must have been some quality in her which held him to the end, and in some queer way he must have been deeply attached to her. Certainly there must have been some good in her which neither his mother nor his friends were able to perceive.... In their private life together, she must have been less cruel than she has been painted."[35]

Unlike the earlier male biographers, Starkie sees some humanity in Duval, but the Irish literary critic also sees Duval as unintelligent and deliberately annoying, "doing all in her power to irritate and exasperate" Baudelaire: "During the early years of their relationship, in a foolish attempt to treat her as an equal, he had tried to educate her in order to make her a more interesting and stimulating companion.... She had proved stupid and incapable of education, and had always expressed contempt for his interests and activities." Later in their relationship, according to Starkie, Duval borrowed money in Baudelaire's name to buy alcohol and drugs; too ashamed to tell his friends that he had been unaware of her actions, he took on the debts. Although Baudelaire hit her and split open her head, Starkie argues that the violence resulted from Duval's actions.[36]

In a 1972 biography, Martin Turnell writes that Baudelaire "selected" Duval "for the part that she was to play in his life, not merely for her looks but for her origin and the colour of her skin. He had come back from the East with his mind stored with memories of an exotic scene, but except for the spectacle of the heaving buttocks of a black woman servant who was being publicly thrashed—a spectacle which had made a powerful impression on him—the scene was empty, and he needed an inhabited scene."[37] Like Frédéric Moreau in *A Sentimental Education*, Baudelaire possessed a type of psychic memory of "heaving black buttocks" that prepared him for his ultimate destiny with Duval. In Turnell's view, "she was chosen partly to enable him to project the morbid element in his attitude towards sexual love—she was the exotic creature whom he could worship and with whom he could indulge in strange practices." In addition, "she was indolent, rapacious, and unfaithful to him with his friends and possibly even with the tradesmen who came to the house."[38]

In a chapter focusing on Baudelaire's "Personal Problems and Literary Beginnings," A. E. Carter's 1977 biography introduces Duval by foregrounding her abhorrent sexuality: "When Baudelaire first met her she was playing walk-on roles in a Latin Quarter theater and earning extra money as a prostitute. Or, more accurately, she was a prostitute who did a little acting. The theater was good advertising; anyone who liked her on the boards had only to step round to the stage door after the performance, she was immediately available." Continuing the onslaught, Carter writes, "She was a common slut, totally uncultivated and extremely stupid; and like most whores she lied with a deliberate, compulsive mendacity which is close to paranoia." Carter further declares that "the verse Baudelaire wrote to Jeanne Duval, to [Apollonie] Sabatier [a white woman with whom Baudelaire was infatuated], and (in a lesser degree) to Marie Daubrun [another actress with whom Baudelaire had a brief liaison], is among the world's greatest erotic poetry. Thanks to this fact a mendacious slut like Jeanne now occupies an unrivaled niche in literature and holds it on her own terms— as a strumpet pure and simple." Carter also notes that both Nadar and Baudelaire cited Duval's "aggressive breasts with their lush contours and pouting nipples."[39] Associating her breasts with "aggression" and "pouting" corrupts her gender identity as simultaneously masculine and feminine.

Carter also repeats the argument that Baudelaire was not at fault for having succumbed to what had long been regarded as the black woman's superhuman sexuality: "One fact emerges from all his poems to her: he understood her very little. Like many men of subtle and profound intelligence, he often missed the obvious. Perhaps he wanted to miss it." Moreover, Carter echoes Starkie's assessment of Duval's intelligence: "Like most whores she was rather pathetic: mentally retarded, slow on the uptake, content to dwell from day to day, tolerant of her queer poet provided he paid the bills." Despite her supposed stupidity, however, she was conniving: she brought to live with her a "lusty brute whose loins were stronger and . . . desires less finicky" than those of Baudelaire and told him that the man "was her brother (most prostitutes have relations of that kind). Baudelaire believed her, and she probably despised him for it. The episode completes her character."[40]

Frederick William John Hemmings's assessment of Duval's "brother" goes beyond the general historical consensus that the man with whom Duval was living was her lover rather than her sibling: because "Baudelaire had been accustomed to her infidelities . . . the discovery of one more could hardly have upset him so violently. What is more likely to have sickened him is that, knowing they were brother and sister (some facial resemblance, or the darkness of the man's complexion, would have been proof enough that they had the same mother at least), he found that they were sleeping together. To speak of incest might have 'scalded his tongue' where ordinary promiscuity would have been accepted with resignation."[41] Duval is thus depicted not merely as a whore but as an incestuous one.

First published in 1985, Anthony Glyn's *The Companion Guide to Paris* offers a vivid and perhaps fanciful description of Baudelaire and Duval's first meeting:

> He would stare at the Seine for hours from his window, and one day he saw, bathing in the river, the beautiful mulatto girl, Jeanne Duval (*La Vénus noire*). (The Seine was relatively unpolluted and bathing was permitted.)
>
> Jeanne's origins are mysterious. She is supposed to have come from the West Indies, and there are conflicting accounts of her appearance: tall, crinkly-haired, graceful, *farouche*, full-breasted, though others have described her as of medium height, ungainly, queen-like and flat-chested. Baudelaire fell passionately in love and

installed her nearby in rue le Regrattier; she became for him the symbol of carnal and profane love.⁴²

Glyn does not provide sources for his account, which diverges from the general consensus that Baudelaire first saw Duval on stage and yet certainly reinscribes the trope of the mysterious black and naked woman.

All of these accounts feature details that seem to have originated somewhere other than in the facts of Duval's life. As Pichois points out, the authors seem to have borrowed "the technique of the novelist seeking to create verisimilitude by the multiplication of 'little, real facts.'" He continues, "The Moral: mistrust excessive details in recollections written down long after the fact by novelists and journalists—as circumstantial excuses or detailed hyperboles that the liar dispenses: too much verisimilitude ends up doing harm."⁴³

Much of this twentieth-century scholarly disdain for Duval stems from the fact that she was an actress, a profession often considered largely synonymous with prostitution. But as historian Lenard Berlanstein points out, nineteenth-century French society considered it acceptable for young bourgeois men to engage in love affairs with actresses, and both Duval and Baudelaire's friends would have seen his overwrought emotional displays as possibly annoying but still appropriate for his status. Further, actresses commonly had a primary, publicly recognized lover who provided financial support as well as other secondary lovers. Baudelaire was not in a position to provide financial support for Duval, meaning that both of them would have expected her to turn to other men. However, relationships or infatuations that developed into excessive or disruptive feelings of love were frowned upon, as were relationships between white men and nonwhite women. Those two characteristics were what made Baudelaire and Duval's relationship unusual.⁴⁴ Though Duval followed the rules for women in the theater, she has been denigrated for her conduct.

Berlanstein also writes that "actresses' oddness, particularly their imputed sexual energy, also required the use of racial construction," including what he describes as a "weaker proclivity for modest behavior and domesticity" that led to "degenerate, primitive" behavior.[45] This existing image of actresses reinforced and strengthened the venom directed at Duval as a consequence of her racial identity and its well-established stereotypes. Such tensions echo those between the metropole (Baudelaire) and the colony (Duval).

CONCLUSION

Baudelaire could not have become a respected white French male intellectual without Duval as his muse. She often inspired his work (though her role is hidden) and thus cannot be ignored in accounts of his life and work. At the same time, his relationship with her—as observed by his friends and family and as depicted in his own letters—clearly demonstrated his failure to live up to what Stoler calls "middle-class morality," "bourgeois sensibilities," and "normalized sexuality."[46] His behavior therefore removed him from the category of authentic white Frenchman. In the wake of his death, his contemporaries and later his biographers sought to reestablish him as a respected white male French intellectual, requiring the development of a narrative that took Duval into account and displaced blame for his failures and shortcomings onto her. And while Duval had no advocates to defend her, the fact that she outlived Baudelaire meant that his contemporaries could not do their damage against her unimpeded. In this small way, Duval pushed back against these depictions and attempts to erase her.

As Stoler writes, "If we accept that 'whiteness' was part of the moral rearmament of bourgeois society," regardless of whether the actors operating within that system acknowledged that fact, "then we need to investigate the nature of that contingent relationship between European racial and class anxieties in the colonies and bourgeois cultivations of self" in France.[47] The treatment of Duval thus holds great symbolic value in light of the end of French slavery.

Duval's tale should be one of an Afro-French girl going about the business of living her life, however banal. Yet according to Baudelaire, his contemporaries, and his biographers, the banality of her life is somehow incongruent with Frenchness. Her association with Baudelaire and particularly her race make her ordinariness extraordinary. Because Baudelaire's defenders could not find a way to incorporate Duval and other black women into the definition of Frenchness, they demonized her and expunged her from the record as much as possible.

CONCLUSION

VÉNUS NOIRE

> Perhaps home is not a place but simply an irrevocable condition.
> —JAMES BALDWIN, *Giovanni's Room*

On 2 October 1925, Josephine Baker appeared in the premiere of *La Danse de sauvage*, costumed only in a skirt made of feathers. The members of the audience at the Théâtre des Champs-Élysées were outraged, delighted, and transfixed. *La Revue nègre* was Paris's newest sensation and Baker the city's brightest new star. Another show—the one for which she perhaps became best known—featured her dancing while wearing only a skirt made of artificial bananas (fig. 25). Dozens of newspapers and journals reported on this iconic "banana dance" and the phallic fruit she wore while jiggling her hips in time with the drum. When the idea of *Danse sauvage* was first presented to writer and director Jacques Charles, he announced, "We need tits. These French people, with their fantasies of black girls, we must give them *des nichons*."[1] This statement neatly encapsulates the long-standing cultural exploitation of and fascination with black women's sexuality. *La Danse de sauvage* presented a curious and mesmerizing sight: an American dancer from St. Louis in a performance choreographed by a Frenchman in an

FIGURE 25.

Josephine Baker, ca. 1926. Josephine Baker performed her renowned *Danse sauvage* garbed in nothing but a skirt made of artificial bananas. Photo by Lucien Waléry (1863–1935).

attempt to represent darkest Africa. For the mere price of a ticket, the masses could see this interpretation of black female sexuality complete with animalistic qualities believed common in African women.

Josephine Baker never claimed Frenchness, although she received great honors from her adopted country. However, Josephine Baker's Americanness mattered little if at all to the white French audiences who watched her from the darkened theater. In performance, her naked black body was manipulated to represent Africa, and she was the quintessential African woman—sexually available and uncivilized, in direct opposition to French self-identity. As Charles so bluntly stated, letting the French see *des nichons* fueled and reinforced French fantasies of black girls.

Despite her brilliance as an entertainer and her subsequent long career, as well as her work with the French Resistance during World War II, Baker never quite escaped such sexualized representations. And it is not clear that she ever wanted to do so—she was an astute businesswoman, too. Baker's enduring popularity in her adopted home highlights the recycling and reuse of nineteenth-century French cultural tropes regarding the hypersexuality and passivity of black women and the primacy of the white male gaze. When I first read Jean-Claude Baker's biography of his mother, I was struck by the amount of apparent rewriting of her history (as well as his own). The mention of *tits* changed the course of my research. *What* fantasies of black girls? What was Charles talking about? I have spent two decades pursuing answers to those questions.

Black women had tremendous cultural impact in nineteenth-century France—an impact that resulted from the racial anxieties first felt in France's black colonies—particularly Saint-Domingue—and exacerbated by the Haitian Revolution. Charles Mills describes the Haitian Revolution as causing an "ontological shudder" among the white polity, threatening the moral and political universe that constructed whites as human and nonwhites as subhuman.[2] This defeat, on the heels of the French Revolution, haunted France throughout the nineteenth century.

White émigrés came back to a France that did not resemble the one they had left. Colonial refugees returned with stories of black barbarism, feeling financially bereft and angry at their government's apparent refusal to assist them in regaining what they had lost. They, too, found a "homeland" that resembled neither where they had come from nor what they remembered. Thus, they were doubly displaced. Finding newly defined French identities would not be painless for any of them.

The loss of Saint-Domingue, often articulated as being at the hands of blacks, had destabilized racial roles. The return of formerly strong and virile French men in the wake of that devastating defeat had unbalanced gender roles. France's resistance to accepting defeat was visible both in its repeated attempts to reclaim its lost colony and in its refusal to call the new nation *Haiti*.

One of the main rhetorical uses for black women in early nineteenth-century France was to mitigate these devastating economic and psychological losses. The black female body provided a canvas that allowed this rhetoric to shore up assertions of French prowess and rearticulate notions of a true (white) French (masculine) national identity. Black women, displaced by both attributes, became reflections of changing attitudes toward race and gender boundaries. France used large-scale racial ventriloquism to ignore slavery, in the process showing precisely how great a social, political, and cultural role it played both in the metropole and in the colonies.

The stories of Sarah Baartmann, Ourika, and Jeanne Duval highlight the myriad ways that the lack of Frenchness could be "proved" when Frenchness was so critical to self and public presentation yet also precarious. It is not surprising that at the end of Restoration, when the wave of French colonial and military supremacy had crested and slavery appeared to have been vanquished, representations of black women returned to those of the ancien régime.

What, then, did it truly mean to be French? If one was white and had lived in the colonies, any racialized identities that had been fostered there had to be sloughed off. These returnees had to embrace a definition implicitly steeped in whiteness. Social constructions of whiteness required constant reminders as well as revisions. These oppositional debates took place not merely in the French imagination but also in both the social and cultural spheres.

Baartmann's body was maligned to "scientifically" prove the superiority of white Frenchness and explain the black female body, thereby demonstrating to white Frenchwomen that they, too, could be controlled. In addition, however, her treatment permitted them to be complicit in new definitions of Frenchness. Representations of Baartmann became a critical guide for subsequent conversations about black female sexuality, restoring prestige to expert white male knowledge and allowing the authority of science to reassert the subjugation of blacks in the metropole. And white Frenchwomen were uplifted in the process.

The story of Ourika, the "perfect" aristocratic young lady, highlighted the strength of race in rendering a person inauthentic within the definitions of Frenchness. At the same time, writing in her voice and dressing like her gave white Frenchmen and -women a unique venue in which to challenge sexual and cultural confinements yet also offered a warning that a failure to assimilate could lead to exile or death.

And Duval, who was integrated into Frenchness through the important benchmarks of language, parentage, and cultural assimilation, became enmeshed in a series of representations that were designed to remove her not only from bourgeois respectability but even from the bohemian milieu. Duval had more ability to "pass" as French—social currency, perhaps based on her skin color as a mixed-race woman—but not class power: she was an actress and prostitute. Though she did contest those narratives to at least some extent, she is known today only because Baudelaire made her legible and because he was famous. Her uneasy life experience also mirrored a France coming to terms with the end of slavery and needing to remake itself in a way that erased blackness along with the institution.

The cultural productions involving these three women contain moments of overlap with their real lives. All were forced into types of prostitution—selling their bodies as commodities. All were caged—literally in Baartmann's case, figuratively in Ourika's and Duval's. And all were "saved" by white French people, allowing viewers to see themselves as saviors. The French could present themselves as a color-blind society despite the fact that race was deeply implicated in everything they did. They employed racial ventriloquism in the invisible territory of the colonies while steadfastly declaring in the metropole that race did not exist. Black women served as their ventriloquist dummies.

As James Baldwin wrote in *Giovanni's Room*, "proving" Frenchness and national belonging is an impossible endeavor.[3] For these women, constantly fighting attempts to render them illegitimate, home simply could not be a place but was an ongoing yet never completed process—except in their own hearts.

The experiences of Sarah Baartmann, Ourika, and Jeanne Duval chipped away at the racial and gender boundaries designed to constrain them, though the effects of their lives may be hard to see directly—like Duval's image in Gustave Courbet's painting. But they are also visible in the life of Josephine Baker, who followed the path they illuminated.

NOTES

INTRODUCTION

1. Cohen, *French Encounter with Africans*, 187.
2. Boulle, *Race et esclavage*, 109.
3. Peabody, "'Nation Born to Slavery.'"
4. See, e.g., the Code Noir of 1685, the law of 30 June 1763 (ordering all blacks to leave France), the law of 19 March 1764 (which gave them permission to remain), and the law of 1777 (which required blacks to register), as well as several 1778 decrees that sought to separate blacks from whites or return blacks to the colonies, to name but a few. Major racial legislation was also enacted in 1716, 1738, and 1762.
5. Peabody, *There Are No Slaves*.
6. See, e.g., Hargreaves, *Immigration, "Race," and Ethnicity*; Noiriel, "National Identity, Nationality, and Citizenship"; Schechter, *Obstinate Hebrews*; Coller, *Arab France*. See also Benedict Anderson, *Imagined Communities*.
7. See, e.g., Milscent, *Sur les Troubles*; Boré, *Faits relatifs aux troubles de Saint-Domingue*; Cocherel, *Observations de M. de Cocherel*; Larchevesque-Thibaud, *Notes sur les troubles de Saint-Domingue*; Page, *Développement des causes des troubles*; Garran de Coulon, *Rapport sur les troubles de Saint-Domingue*; Raymond [Raimond], *Réflexions sur les véritables causes des troubles*.
8. Popkin, *Facing Racial Revolution*, 366.
9. Sepinwall, "Specter of Saint-Domingue," 326.
10. See Cohen, *French Encounter with Africans*, 181; see also Jennings, *French Anti-Slavery*, 81.
11. Sepinwall, "Specter of Saint-Domingue," 324.
12. Kumar, "English and French National Identity," 415.

13. See Meadows, "Planters of Saint-Domingue."

14. Ibid.

15. Smalls, "Slavery Is a Woman."

16. This book is also informed by the belief that colonial experiences shaped the colony and metropole equally and thus are "inseparable," with reciprocal transformative effects. See Cobban, *History of Modern France*, 39; Frederick Cooper and Stoler, "Between Metropole and Colony," 1–3, 16.

17. Marie-Guillemine Benoist was born into the aristocracy. She was a professional painter who studied under Jacques-Louis David (one of three women chosen to receive instruction). Some critics argued that she did not paint the canvas, believing its style more reminiscent of David's "masculinist" style. Others believed that the race of the subject of her painting "tainted" Benoist—a point developed throughout this study. See also Smalls, "Slavery Is a Woman."

18. Pollock writes that the "negress" was either an African or African Caribbean whom "her sailor brother-in-law had brought back to France from the Antilles" (*Differencing the Canon*, 297).

19. Ibid.; Lévy, *Marie-Guillemine Laville-Leroulx et les siens*. Denise Murrell, the curator of *Le Modèle noire de Géricault à Matisse* (The Black Model from Géricault to Matisse), an exhibit at the Musée d'Orsay in Paris, France, in 2019, renamed the painting *Portrait of Madeleine* for the exhibition. The painting was also exhibited under that name in New York (where the exhibit was titled *Posing Modernity: The Black Model from Manet and Matisse to Today*). It is unknown whether the Louvre will keep this name when the painting is returned to its collections. See https://www.musee-orsay.fr/en/events/exhibitions/in-the-museums/exhibitions-in-the-musee-dorsay-more/article/le-modele-noir-47692.html?tx_ttnews%5Btx_pids%5D=591&tx_ttnews%5Btt_cur%5D=47692&tx_ttnews%5BbackPid%5D=223&cHash=2a810ca93e.

20. Albigès, "Portrait d'une négresse."

21. Honour and Fleming, *World History of Art*, 642–43.

22. Eichthal and Urbain, *Lettres sur la race noire et la race blanche*, 22.

23. Ghosh, *Sex and the Family*, makes a compelling argument connecting cohabitation between British men and Indian women and the early British imperial government's anxieties about Britishness and Indianness. I am interested in how some of the issues about national belonging play out in the metropole.

24. Gilroy, *Black Atlantic*, 4. Gilroy writes specifically about England, but his point applies to France as well.

25. Many studies of French national identity concentrate on the state's effort to construct and deploy a national identity through institutions such as univer-

sal primary schooling and conscription. Others focus on the role of warfare and antagonisms such as the Franco-German dynamic initiated by the Franco-Prussian War of 1870–71. See Bell, *Cult of the Nation*. See also Hobsbawm, *Nations and Nationalism*. Few studies, however, have examined changing French conceptions of national identity between 1800 and 1848, when slavery was finally abolished. See Coller, *Arab France*.

26. Hunt, *Family Romance*, xiv.

27. Hesse, *Other Enlightenment*.

28. Several texts put women in the forefront, including Arlette Gautier, *Les Sœurs de solitude*; Moitt, *Women and Slavery*; Palmer, *Intimate Bonds*. Studies of orientalist discourse as France's colonial gaze turned toward North Africa and the Middle East include Sessions, *By Sword and Plow*. In *The Family and the Nation*, Heuer rightly admonishes scholars for neglecting gender; however, she argues that women's "national and citizenship status was more urgent in the colonies throughout the nineteenth century, since racial hierarchies explicitly overlaid—and sometimes opposed—'national' differences" (200). She does not, however, speak about how racial hierarchies might have moved into France from the colonies when those women and men came back. In *France after Revolution*, Davidson makes some relevant and provocative arguments regarding the "confusion about gender, class, and sexuality, as well as the political and social significance of the family [that] reverberated through French society in the wake of the Revolution" (4), but she does not include any sustained treatment of race. This absence is curious, since she also argues that "interactions between people and ideas in urban social spaces enabled heterogeneous groups to observe each other, learn from what they saw, and thus construct notions of their own identity and how that identity differed from that of others around them" (6). Davidson and Heuer have incorporated gender into their analyses, arguing that crucial divisions surrounding class, sexuality, and gender emerged during the postrevolutionary and Restoration eras. In doing so, they have opened up a space to more clearly see how these past events impacted both men and women living during such profound historical moments.

29. For representations of black women in literature, see Hoffmann, *Le Nègre romantique*; Fanoudh-Seifer, *Le Mythe du nègre*; Jean-Claude Blachère, *Le Modèle Nègre*; Sharpley-Whiting, *Black Venus*. For art, see Doy, "More Than Meets the Eye"; Chalaye, *Du Noir au nègre*. See also Grigsby, *Extremities*; Grigsby, "Revolutionary Sons."

30. See, e.g., Stovall and Van den Abbeele, *French Civilization and Its Discontents*; Chapman and Frader, *Race in France*; Peabody and Stovall, *Color of Liberty*; Prasad, *Colonialism*; Fogarty, *Race and War in France*; Ezra, *Colonial*

Unconscious; Silverstein, *Algeria in France*; Hargreaves, *Immigration,* "*Race*" *and Ethnicity*.

31. See esp. Smalls, "Slavery Is a Woman"; Grigsby, *Extremities*; Sharpley-Whiting, *Black Venus*.

32. Important parallel studies include Garraway, *Libertine Colony*; Miller, *French Atlantic Triangle*; Dobie, *Trading Places*.

33. Fuentes, *Dispossessed Lives*, 5.

34. Said, *Orientalism*, 2–3.

35. Darnton, "Early Information Society."

36. Daniels and Cosgrove posit that "while, by definition, all art history translates the visual into the verbal, the iconographic approach consciously sought to conceptualise pictures as encoded texts to be deciphered by those cognisant of the culture as a whole in which they were produced" ("Introduction," 2). See also Poole, *Vision, Race, and Modernity*.

37. No record has been found of the original name of the woman known variously as Saartje Bartmann, Sarah Baartmann, and Sarah Bartmann (the version under which she was baptized). Except when quoting other sources, I use *Sarah Baartmann*, which is the currently accepted spelling.

CHAPTER 1. THE TALE OF THREE WOMEN

1. "African Venus," Walters Art Museum.

2. Similarly, the name of the woman shown in *Portrait d'une femme noire* (see fig. 2) was not recorded even though her mistress painted her and must have known it. See note 19 to the introduction.

3. Smalls argues that Cordier and other artists did not record their subjects' names in an attempt to universalize the images ("Exquisite Empty Shells," 293–94). See also "Facing the Other."

4. Gilman, "Black Bodies, White Bodies," in *"Race," Writing, and Difference*, 223. In the introduction to *Black Venus*, Sharpley-Whiting takes Gilman to task, mainly for his lack of nuance concerning Baartmann. I agree with this assessment; however, I believe that Gilman remains required reading when attempting to explore the correlation between blackness and whiteness in Europe, and seeing how others used Baartmann's image remains a useful endeavor.

5. Little, "Le Nom et les origines d'Ourika." See also De Raedt, "Representations of the Real-Life Ourika," 57–65; De Raedt, "Ourika en noir et blanc."

6. See Sabran and Boufflers, *La Comtesse de Sabran et le Chevalier de Boufflers*. See also Crofts, "Duras's Ourika," 135; De Raedt, "Ourika: L'Inspiration"; De Raedt, "Ourika in Black and White."

7. Stanislas Jean de Boufflers to Mme. de Sabran, 8 February 1786, in Sabran and Boufflers, *La Comtesse de Sabran et le Chevalier de Boufflers*, 101, translation mine.

8. Stanislas Jean de Boufflers to Mme. de Sabran, 19 July 1786, in ibid., 218–20, translation mine. See also Kadish and Massardier-Kenney, *Translating Slavery* (1994), 189.

9. See Rouillard, "Black Galatea," 210.

10. Mme. de Sabran to Stanislas Jean de Boufflers, 26 July, in Maugras and Croze-Lemercier, *Delphine de Sabran, marquise de Custine*, 27, translation mine.

11. McCloy, *Negro in France*, 30.

12. Lowe, "Stereotyping of Black Africans," 23–24.

13. McCloy, *Negro in France*, 30.

14. Ibid.; Debrunner, *Presence and Prestige*, 100.

15. Bonneserre de Saint-Denis, *Revue historique, nobiliaire et biographique*, vol. 9, 349, s.v. "Ourika (Charlotte-Catherine-Benezet)."

16. Little, "Peau noire, masque blanc" ("Black Skin, White Mask"), vii, translation mine; De Raedt, "Representations of the Real-Life Ourika," 57. Little does not cite sources in his preface to this edition of *Ourika*, making it difficult to analyze the validity of his assertions.

17. Sophie de Tott, *Ourika*, ca. 1793, from the frontispiece of Duras, *Ourika*. The girl in the painting looks too young to be Ourika, who would have been about thirteen in 1793, though Tott might have been depicting how Ourika appeared as a child.

18. See De Raedt, "Representations of the Real-Life Ourika," 60.

19. La Tour du Pin, *Journal d'une femme de cinquante ans*, 184, translation mine.

20. "Avis de parens de la mineure Ourika," Archives Départementales Paris, "État des pièces remises au directeur des domaines nationaux de l'intérieur de Paris formant la totalité de celles déposées aux Archives des Domaines National du département de la Seine provenant de la succession en desherence de Charlotte Catherine Benezet, négresse qui demeuroit chez la c[itoy]enne Beauveau rue du faubourg Honoré," No. 44f Division du Roule Depot No. 3685, Year VIII, Archives Départementales, Paris, DQ(10)461, pièce 106, Year III. This document was originally found at the Archives Nationales but can also be found at the Archives de la Seine, Paris, as "Certifié véritable le pouvoir de l'autre part," DI U(1)2, no. 87, and DQ 10, 1443, pièce 3014, Year III.

21. Ibid. Pierre Boulle to author, March 2017.

22. Peabody, "Ourika in the History Classroom," 125; "État des pièces remises au directeur des domaines nationaux de l'intérieur de Paris formant la total-

ité de celles déposées aux Archives des Domaines National du département de la Seine provenant de la succession en desherence de Charlotte Catherine Benezet, négresse qui demeuroit chez la c[itoy]enne Beauveau rue du faubourg Honoré," No. 44f Division du Roule Depot No. 3685, Year VIII, Archives Départementales, Paris, DQ(10)461, pièce 106. This document is also found at the Archives de la Seine as T1688, no. 3442, but Ourika is listed as "Benezel," not as "Benezet." The current location of Ourika's body is unclear. Her benefactors were originally buried on their estate, but the bodies were subsequently moved, first to the old cemetery in Saint-Germain and later to the newer cemetery.

23. Letters from Mme. de Beauvau, 21 July, 27 January 1799, in Beauvau, *Souvenirs de la Maréchale Princesse de Beauvau*, 148, translation mine.

24. Ibid., 147–48, translations mine.

25. Ibid., 147, 150, 149, 150, translations mine.

26. Crais and Scully, *Sara Baartman and the Hottentot Venus*, 184n1. Kirby asserts that she was born around 1788, somewhere within the boundaries of Caffraria, to the West of Great Fish River ("More about the Hottentot Venus," 128). Most historians have accepted Kirby's argument; for example, see Sharpley-Whiting, "Dawning of Racial-Sexual Science," 116. But Crais and Scully contend that most of the overarching narrative repeated by scholars about Baartmann is incorrect, and I find these arguments persuasive. Anxiety over interracial relationships and the proliferation of multiracial children in the French colonies led to a fanaticism regarding the development of racial categorizations. As a result, these narratives needed to emphasize Baartmann's alleged eroticism to make her seem sexually repulsive, thereby perpetuating the social disdain for mixing of the races. For Baartmann's importance to scientific racism and to nineteenth-century constructions of race, see Blainville, "Sur une Femme"; Cuvier, "Extrait d'observations." For a terrific scientific, race, and gender analysis, see Fausto-Sterling, "Gender, Race, and Nation." See also Abrahams, "Images of Sara Baartmann"; Wiss, "Lipreading." For useful information on Baartmann and other blacks, see Lindfors "'Hottentot Venus' and Other African Attractions"; Lindfors, "Ethnological Show Business"; Fauvelle-Aymar, *L'Invention du hottentot*; Badou, *L'Énigme de la Vénus hottentote*. Finally, a 1998 film, *The Life and Times of Sara Baartmann*, by South African documentarian Zola Maseko, uses new archival research to expand our overall knowledge of Baartmann as a South African woman sold into a different kind of bondage to serve the financial, social, and erotic needs of her new "keepers."

27. Crais and Scully, *Sara Baartman and the Hottentot Venus*, 38, 43–45.

28. Cesars's name also appears as *Cesar* and *Caesar*.

29. Kirby, "More about the Hottentot Venus," 125; Kirby, "Hottentot Venus," 55; Crais and Scully, *Sara Baartman and the Hottentot Venus*, 54–57, 59, 61; Sharpley-Whiting, "Dawning of Racial-Sexual Science," 117; Lindfors, "'Hottentot Venus' and Other African Attractions," 86. For more on the contract, which has been the source of considerable scholarly debate, see sworn deposition of the court signed by Samuel Solly, representative for Zachary Macaulay, and John George Moojen, representative for Alexander Dunlop and Henrick Caesar, 28 November 1810, Record PFF 723 (J18/462), Public Records Office, London. Crais and Scully assert that Dunlop and Cesar signed a contract in the Cape and that Baartmann was not a party to any agreement; in addition, they argue, she was listed as free. But since she was not involved in the contract, she clearly was not free, and the validity of the court documents is thus called into question. Kirby believes that the contract was a fraud, written after Baartmann arrived in London and attracted attention from abolitionists. Solly and Moojen's deposition states that she was to be "Caesar's nursery maid" and that the period of servitude was six years ("Following Is the Result," 41–42), while a sworn statement by William Bullock gives the time as two years (William Bullock, "In the Kings Bench," 21 November 1810, Record PFF 723 [J18/462], Public Records Office, London) and other court documents say five years. Dunlop apparently sold his stake in Baartmann after reaching London.

30. *The Times*, 26 November 1810, 3.

31. Ibid. Abolitionists seized on her countenance as a way to prove she was being held against her will. See "Transcripts of the Sworn Affidavits Filed during the Trial of 1810," deposition of Zachary Macaulay, Thomas Gisborne-Babington, and Peter Van Wageninge, October 17, 1810, Record PFF 747 (KB1/36/4, f. 117), Public Records Office, London, under "Saartjie Baartman on Display" (also Issue 8150 Col. B. "Under Law Report" Court of King's Bench), http://www.nationalarchives.gov.uk/pathways/blackhistory/culture/transcripts/baartman_display.htm.

32. Mathews, *Memoirs of Charles Mathews, Comedian*, 4:137.

33. Ibid., 137, 138. According to Crais and Scully, *Sara Baartman and the Hottentot Venus*, 80, Cesars threatened Baartmann if she did not comply with his orders to perform.

34. Mathews, *Memoirs of Charles Mathews, Comedian*, 4:136.

35. "Transcripts of the Sworn Affidavits"; Solly and Moojen, "Following Is the Result," 41–42. See also "Curiosities and Exhibits." Crais and Scully note that Macaulay did nothing to assist the two enslaved black boys, probably because he had been a slave overseer in Jamaica and did not want to bring attention to his own past issues (*Sara Baartman and the Hottentot Venus*, 87–89).

36. Solly and Moojen, "Following Is the Result."

37. "Transcripts of the Sworn Affidavits," 45.

38. Kirby, "More about the Hottentot Venus," 128. For more on Baartmann's time in England, see Crais and Scully, *Sara Baartman and the Hottentot Venus*, esp. chaps. 3–5. According to Holmes, Baartmann folded the certificate and carried it with her until she died (*African Queen*, 95). Although Holmes is prone to attributing intense emotions to Baartmann without citing the sources from which that information was obtained, I believe that Holmes has correctly assessed the certificate's importance to Baartmann.

39. Crais and Scully, *Sara Baartman and the Hottentot Venus*, 199n15, 119. Citing an article from the *Manchester Mercury*, Crais and Scully suggest that Baartmann may have married Dunlop and become pregnant. Cohen says she died of tuberculosis (*French Encounter with Africans*, 239). According to Lindfors, she had smallpox that was misdiagnosed by the doctor who treated her ("'Hottentot Venus' and Other African Attractions," 89). According to Crais and Scully, Parisian newspapers published more obituaries for Baartmann than for any other nineteenth-century African woman (*Sara Baartman and the Hottentot Venus*, 138).

40. Higginbotham asserts that "gender itself was both constructed and fragmented by race. Gender, so colored by race, remained from birth until death inextricably linked to one's personal identity and social status. For black and white women, gendered identity was reconstructed and represented in very different, indeed antagonistic, racialized contexts" ("African-American Women's History," 258).

41. Gilman, "Black Bodies, White Bodies," *"Race," Writing, and Difference*, 225.

42. Gilman, "Black Sexuality and Modern Consciousness," 112.

43. Sharpley-Whiting, *Black Venus*, 17.

44. Mosse, *Toward the Final Solution*, 15. See also Bindman, *Ape to Apollo*.

45. "There were by the late eighteenth century established opinions on these matters, combining religious traditions and philosophical ideas on the 'chain of being,' human nature, and history, with new theories and techniques of classification in natural and social science. In our period this was expanded, altered, and elaborated by the use of a rapidly growing body of empirical and descriptive material produced by European visitors to non-European societies, but also by the development of the 'scientific' disciplines of biology, ethnology, and anthropology" (De Groot, "'Sex' and 'Race,'" 95).

46. Gilman, "Black Bodies, White Bodies," in *"Race," Writing, and Difference*, 231.

47. The very earliest modern invocation of race in French writing, from the late seventeenth century, posited Hottentots as a race apart from other Africans and associated them with "ugliness." See Boulle, "François Bernier," 11–27; [Bernier], "Nouvelle Division de la terre par les différentes espèces ou races qui l'habitent," 133–44.

48. Gilman, *Difference and Pathology*, 112.

49. See Blumenbach, "Degeneration of the Races," 79–90; Cuvier, "The Race from Which We Are Descended Has Been Called Caucasian," 104–8.

50. "Nouvelles de Paris," *La Quotidienne*, 1 January 1816, 4, translation mine.

51. Cuvier, "Extraits d'observation," 265, 159, translations mine; Sharpley-Whiting, *Black Venus*, 27.

52. Sharpley-Whiting, 30; Cuvier, "Extrait d'observations," 266–69, 273, translations mine.

53. Ibid., 263; Blainville, "Sur une Femme de la race hottentote," 189, translation mine; Fausto-Sterling, "Gender, Race, and Nation," 36. Blainville doubted some of the assertions of sexual aggression.

54. Fausto-Sterling, "Gender, Race, and Nation," 42.

55. See Pollock, *Differencing the Canon*, 309n40. Pichois's research on Jeanne Duval has connected her to "Berthe" and lists her as a quadroon (*Baudelaire: Études et témoignages*, 72).

56. Hemmings, *Baudelaire the Damned*, 50; Pichois, *Baudelaire*, trans. Robb, 203–4. According to Hemmings, Duval was "almost certainly born on the Guinea coast, where she had the misfortune to be taken captive and sold into slavery. In the eighteenth century French traders who for one reason or another found they could not sell a female slave . . . sometimes shipped them to Nantes where they disposed of them to brothel-keepers. Apparently, this was the fate of the miserable black girl, Jeanne's grandmother, whose owners had chosen to name her Marie Duval." According to Jacques Crépet, Jeanne's mother's death certificate lists the name *Lemer* or *Lemaire* and says that she died on 15 November 1853 at the age of sixty-three ("Une Femme à Enterrer," Acte de décès, Jeanne Lemaire, 151–52). Even if her grandmother was from Saint-Domingue, Duval's paternal lineage means that she should have been classified as a quadroon or octoroon rather than a mulatto.

57. Baudelaire to his mother, 27 March 1852, as quoted in Dolan, "Skirting the Issue," Dolan's translation, 613. Baudelaire frequently uses underlining and capital letters to add emphasis in his letters.

58. See Angela Carter, *Black Venus's Tale*; Hopkinson, *Salt Roads*; Maud Sulter's exhibition about Jeanne Duval, *Jeanne Duval: A Melodrama*, 30 May–

31 August 2003, Scottish National Portrait Gallery. For comments on Carter's take, see Tonkin, "Musing on Baudelaire"; Munford, "Re-Presenting Charles Baudelaire/Re-Presenting Jeanne Duval."

59. Nadar, *Charles Baudelaire*, 7–12; Wilson, *Bohemians*, 85, 92; Berlanstein, *Daughters of Eve*, 63, 24. For more on bohemians, see Seigel, *Bohemian Paris*. Pichois disputes many of Nadar's recollections, including his claim to have met Duval before Baudelaire did ("A Propos d'un Poème de Baudelaire," 193; *Baudelaire: Études et témoignages*, 75).

60. Starkie, *Baudelaire*, 84; Pichois, *Baudelaire: Études et témoignages*, 63. Pichois has done a thorough job of finding the productions that Jeanne was alleged to have appeared in. However, scholars are uncertain whether she appeared in productions on certain dates, and there were multiple productions.

61. Starkie, *Baudelaire*, 84. See also Pichois, *Baudelaire: Études et témoignages*, 73, translation mine.

62. Baudelaire, *Letters of Charles Baudelaire to His Mother*, trans. Symons, 13.

63. Weissmann, *Darwin's Audubon*, 287.

64. Pichois, *Baudelaire: Études et témoignages*, 79, translation mine; Baudelaire to Narcisse Désiré Ancelle, 30 June 1845, in Baudelaire, *Correspondance générale*, 1:70, translation mine. Baudelaire later accused Ancelle of flirting with Duval (Christophe, "Jeanne Duval," 434).

65. Baudelaire to his mother, 26 March 1853, in *Selected Letters of Charles Baudelaire*, trans. Lloyd, 56–57.

66. Baudelaire to his mother, 18 November 1853, in Pichois, *Baudelaire*, trans. Robb, 202; see also *Letters of Charles Baudelaire to His Mother*, trans. Symons, 58.

67. Baudelaire to his mother, 11 September 1856, in Baudelaire, *Letters of Charles Baudelaire to His Mother*, trans. Symons, 94.

68. Jacques Crépet believes that she was actually at least thirty-four at this time ("Charles Baudelaire et Jeanne Duval," *La Plume*, 15 April 1898, 242–43, translation mine). It is possible that someone else provided this information to the hospital or that Duval lied about her age and birthplace.

69. Baudelaire to his mother, 17 March 1861, in Baudelaire, *Letters of Charles Baudelaire to His Mother*, trans. Symons, 199.

70. Baudelaire to his mother, 6 May 1861, in ibid., 176, 178; Baudelaire to Ancelle, 1 April 1861, in Baudelaire, *Selected Letters of Charles Baudelaire*, trans. Lloyd, 164; Richon, *Jeanne Duval et Charles Baudelaire*, 164.

71. Pichois, *Baudelaire*, trans. Robb, 168; Richon, *Jeanne Duval et Charles Baudelaire*, 25. It is unclear whether Duval sat for Courbet; Baudelaire's likeness was taken from an earlier image.

72. Calvé, *Sous Tous les Ciels*, 140–42, translation mine.

73. Richon made exhaustive attempts to find her grave and death record, to no avail (*Jeanne Duval et Charles Baudelaire*, 160).

74. McClintock, *Imperial Leather*, 209.

CHAPTER 2. ENTERING DARKNESS

1. Eliel, "Louis-Léopold Boilly's 'The Galleries of the Palais-Royal.'"

2. Rétif de la Bretonne, *Palais-Royal*, 1:164–72. Rétif de la Bretonne tells a compelling (though perhaps not accurate) story regarding "cette belle noire" ("this beautiful black girl," 164) that involves rape, murder, transport aboard a ship from Africa to France, the death of her mother, and her ultimate purchase and enslavement.

3. According to Eliel, the hats worn by Esther and her companion indicate that they are of a higher class of prostitute, possibly under the guardianship of a brothel ("Louis-Léopold Boilly's 'The Galleries of the Palais-Royal,'" 279n31).

4. Ibid., 279.

5. For the trauma of this era, see Kroen, *Politics and Theater*, 20; Gildea, *Children of the Revolution*, 1–2; Stewart, *Restoration Era in France*, 10; Austin, *1815*, 15.

6. For many years, historians of the postrevolutionary and Restoration periods in France largely overlooked the question of race; however, more recent works that have explored race and slavery during this era include Cohen, *French Encounter with Africans*; Jennings, *French Anti-Slavery*; Jennings, *French Reaction*; Heuer, *Family and the Nation*; Boulle and Peabody, *Droit des noirs*.

7. Cohen, *French Encounter with Africans*, 205.

8. Kwon, "'Remember Saint Domingue,'" 24.

9. Colnet, "Sartjée; ou, La Vénus hottentot à son cousin," 2:50–67.

10. I searched the *Journal de l'empire* and its index for all of 1814.

11. Montesquieu, *Lettres persanes*, letter 30, "Comment peut-on être Persan?"; I cite Montesquieu, *Persian Letters*, trans. Mauldon, 40.

12. Howland, *Letter Form*, 117, 133.

13. See Childs, "Black Exotic"; Grigsby, *Extremities*, esp. chap. 6.

14. Colnet, "Sartjée; ou, La Vénus hottentot à son cousin," 50, translation mine.

15. Ibid., 51–52.

16. Ibid., 52.

17. Ibid., 52–53 and 56–57. In eighteenth-century France, there were many satires (pornographic and otherwise) of Marie Antoinette's hair. The satirists made her already tall hairstyles even bigger, adding such nonsensical things

as a table and chairs and ships, a phenomenon that is likely related to exposing women's attempts at political life as frivolous pursuits. See Hunt, *Family Romance*, 89–123.

18. Colnet, "Sartjée; ou, La Vénus hottentot à son cousin," 58, translations mine.

19. Ibid., 59.

20. Ibid., 60.

21. Ibid., 61.

22. Ibid., 61, 64.

23. See Burrows, *French Exile*.

24. Colnet, "Sartjée; ou, La Vénus hottentot à son cousin," 65–66, translation mine.

25. Davis, *Disability Studies Reader*, 7.

26. Théaulon, Dartois, and Brasier, *Vénus hottentote*. The English translation of the play is available in its entirety in the appendix to Sharpley-Whiting, *Black Venus*; all English quotations are taken from this edition.

27. "Première Représentation de la Vénus hottentote," *Journal des débats politiques et littéraires*, 21 November 1814, 3–4, translation mine. See also Strother, "Display of the Body Hottentot."

28. *Gazette de France*, 21 November 1814, translation mine; Strother, "Display of the Body Hottentot," 54n56.

29. Divorce was first allowed in France during the revolution. Given that the production takes place in presumably real time (1814), Adolphe's wives must have wasted no time in cheating.

30. "The *Hottentot Venus*; or, *Hatred* of Frenchwomen," in Sharpley-Whiting, *Black Venus*, 150, 160–61; "le peuple où les femmes sont le plus renommées par leur beauté" (Théaulon, Dartois, and Brasier, *Vénus hottentote*, 30).

31. "The *Hottentot Venus*; or, *Hatred* of Frenchwomen," in Sharpley-Whiting, *Black Venus*, 162–64.

32. Ibid., 130.

33. Ibid., 153.

34. *Journal des dames et des modes*, 25 January 1815, 37–40.

35. Ibid., 37–38.

36. Ibid., 38–39.

37. Ibid., 39.

38. Ibid.

39. Ibid., 39–40.

40. See, for example, Popkin, *Facing Racial Revolution*.

41. Tanner, *History*, 162–63. Tanner is summarizing the work of nineteenth-century French doctor and economist Louis-René Villermé. According to Tanner, "In all France, Villermé found that conscripts taller than 165 cm. (5 feet, 1 inch) constituted 45 per cent of the total in 1816–17 and 50 percent in 1826–27, with a regular increase in between," which suggests a taller national average, though it is difficult to compare (163). I thank Sue Peabody for leading me to this information.

42. Cresswell, *Oxford Dictionary of Word Origins*, 43. See also "Why Do the French Call the British 'the Roast Beefs'?" For Sharpley-Whiting's take on the significance of this print, see *Black Venus*, 21.

43. Fields, *Intimate Affair*, 124. See also Sharpley-Whiting, *Black Venus*; Pieterse, *White on Black*; McClintock, *Imperial Leather*.

44. Crais and Scully, *Sara Baartman and the Hottentot Venus*, 147.

45. See Popkin, *Facing Racial Revolution*.

CHAPTER 3. OURIKA MANIA

1. "Review of New Books: *Ourika by the Duchess de Duras*," *London Literary Gazette*, 22 May 1824. Literary and historical scholars have recently taken renewed interest in *Ourika*. See, among others, Birkett and Rivers, *Approaches to Teaching Duras's Ourika*; Tuori, "Femme déracinée"; Romanowski, *Through Strangers' Eyes*; Taormina, "*L'Ourika* de Claire de Duras"; Mignogna, "Ourika."

2. Merton, *Literary Magnet*, 3.

3. Sollors, *Neither Black nor White*, 345; Crofts, "Duras's Ourika," 152–55. As many as six plays may have been written, but the names of only four survive. In England, articles on Ourika appeared in *Literary Gazette*, 17 January, 22, 29 May, 5 June, 21 August 1824; *Kaleidoscope*, 1, 15, 22 June 1824; *Lady's Monthly Museum*, July 1824. In the United States, writing about Ourika appeared in *Atlantic*, 1 October 1824; *United States Literary Gazette*, 15 October 1824; and the *New-York Mirror*, 29 January 1825, 23 July 1831.

4. See Kafer, *Feminist, Queer, Crip*; Clare, *Exile and Pride*; Schalk, "Metaphorically Speaking"; Schalk, "Coming to Claim Crip"; Davis, *Enforcing Normalcy*. For more on the medical connotations of *mania*, see, e.g., Martin, *Bipolar Expeditions*; Davis, *Bending over Backwards*. While I use *Ourika Mania* to describe and analyze this specific historical moment, I do not intend to propagate the phrase's legitimacy or reinforce it as an appropriate label: it is not. I am simply borrowing the term used in historical context.

5. Martin, *Bipolar Expeditions*, 19.

6. Boulle and Peabody, *Droit des noirs*, 191–93, 205.

7. I looked at every 1824 issue of the *Journal des débats politiques et littéraires*, one of the most important journals of the Restoration.

8. Quoted in Duras, *Ourika*, ed. Little, 98.

9. Chalaye, *Les Ourika du boulevard*, xv.

10. For the debate on whether she went to Martinique, see Miller, *French Atlantic Triangle*, 160.

11. Kale, *French Salons*, 180; Sharpley-Whiting, "Black Blood, White Masks," 52–53; Duras, *Ourika*, trans. Fowles, viii. See also Kadish and Massardier-Kenney, *Translating Slavery* (2010), 188. For an overview of the novel's publication status and editions, see Crofts, "Duras's Ourika," 91–96. Duras's Ourika may have been at least partially based on another young foreigner, Aïssé, known as La Belle Circassienne (Ransom, "Mademoiselle Aïssé," 84). However, despite the similarities between the two women, they were of different races. Boom suggests similarities between Ourika and a heroine from a seventeenth-century French novel ("Monkey-Girls of Old Regime France"). Peabody suggests that Duras may have met the real Ourika ("Ourika in the History Classroom," 126).

12. Duras, *Ourika*, trans. Fowles, 7–10.

13. Ibid., 12–14.

14. Rushforth makes a similar argument in *Bonds of Alliance*.

15. Duras, *Ourika*, trans. Fowles, 15–16.

16. However, Fowles's assessment that it constitutes "this first serious attempt by a white novelist to enter a black mind" seems a disturbing allusion to racial essentialism (ibid., xxx). There is no such thing as a monolithic mindset based on race or any other category: a claim that a work entered the "Jewish mind," for example, would provoke an instant (and deserved) backlash. Moreover, as Alyssa Sepinwall points out, the novel "purports to be an African woman's voice, but is instead that of a white aristocrat in the post-revolutionary era" (quoted in Peabody, "Ourika in the History Classroom," 126).

17. Duras, *Ourika*, trans. Fowles, 42, 43, 17–18.

18. For the importance of marriage for French aristocracy and the taboo of miscegenation, see Woshinsky, "Teachings of *Ourika*," 157–61; Chilcoat, "Civility, Marriage, and the Impossible French Citizen," 125–44.

19. Miller, *French Atlantic Triangle*, 158–59 (*Ourika* was a "startling modern commentary on race"; "what it says about slavery has been largely ignored"; and the novel is a "critique on [Duras's] own class"); Prasad, *Colonialism, Race, and the French Romantic Imagination*, 102. Prasad also writes, "To be sure, it would be erroneous to claim that Ourika's blackness is just a structural variation within the master plots of sentimental and Romantic alienation, one that

could be easily replaced with 'class' or 'sexuality.' Nor would it be entirely correct to say that the novel's treatment of race is without a social project of emancipation. Rather, the erasures I have highlighted in the plot of the novel point to the inadequacy of discussing race as a broad category of identity, without full attention to the specific components that constitute Ourika's subjectivity. Ourika occupies the impossible position of a black European aristocrat. This position is further complicated by her gender, for, as a woman, her social integration is predicated upon her marriageability" (108–9). See also Ingersoll, "Appropriation of Black Experience." According to Ingersoll, "Ourika may be lent the author-ity [sic] to tell her own story, but those who appropriate that story for their own purposes, however praiseworthy those purposes may be, render this text a problematical representation of black experience" (2).

20. O'Connell, "*Ourika*," 47.

21. For more on the refugee narrative of racial victimization, see Meadows, "Planters of Saint-Domingue"; Brady, "Recovering."

22. Brady, "Recovering," 53.

23. Jenson, "Mirror Insurrections," 46.

24. O'Connell, "*Ourika*," 50. O'Connell states that Duras's work was more concerned with psychological than social issues, though the two may be inseparable in this case. See also Jenson, "Mirror Insurrections," 46.

25. Jenson, "Mirror Insurrections," 45–50.

26. Duras, *Ourika*, trans. Fowles, 20, 22, 24, 39.

27. Ibid., 21.

28. Kelly takes this idea even further, writing that "[n]o matter how exceptional Ourika is, how well brought up and educated, she cannot escape the social machine that defines her as a nonaristocratic black woman—a person with no social or economic capital, nothing to give to any prospective family" ("*Ourika*," 88).

29. Bertrand-Jennings, "*Ourika*," 76. Fay, "He Said, She Said," 145–50, voices a similar view. Kelly writes that Ourika "does not reject her society; rather, she mourns the fact that she is not able to be included in it" ("*Ourika*," 89).

30. O'Connell, "*Ourika*," 49.

31. Crofts, "Duras's Ourika," 99, 117–18.

32. Kadish and Massardier-Kenney, *Translating Slavery* (2010), 189n8. Crofts, "Duras's Ourika," 165, calls the names "affectionate," but that seems highly unlikely, particularly since *bourika* is slang for "donkey."

33. According to Crofts, women writers faced the additional problem that

their work was seen as autobiographical, an issue that would have been especially acute for Duras given that her protagonist was a black and thus an inauthentic aristocrat ("Duras's Ourika," 100–104).

34. Ibid., 5.

35. Ibid., 155.

36. "Modes," *Le Diable boiteux*, 25 May 1824, 4, translation mine.

37. "The *Hottentot Venus*; or, *Hatred* of Frenchwomen," in Sharpley-Whiting, *Black Venus*, 138.

38. Sollors, *Neither Black nor White*, 345. I have found no additional information about Ourika food products other than they were said to have existed, and I have not found advertisements for such products in French journals or newspapers.

39. In addition to these Parisian productions, a one-act musical was published in Scotland. See Perry, *Ourika, the Orphan of Senegal*. For analyses of the literary and theatrical merit of these texts, see Cowles, "Subjectivity of the Colonial Subject," 29–43; Chilcoat, "Confinement," 6–16; DiMauro, "Ourika," 187; O'Connell, "Ourika," 47–56; Rouillard, "Black Galatea," 207–22; Warburton, "Ashes, Ashes," 165–86. See also Barbara T. Cooper, "Staging Ourika," 97–113; Cheyne, "Love No Other." None of these productions was well received by critics or audiences. See Chalaye, *Les Ourika du boulevard*, introduction.

40. "Ourika; ou, La Négresse," in Chalaye, *Les Ourika du boulevard*, 13, translation mine.

41. Ibid., 15–17, translation mine.

42. Ibid., 47, 42, 59, 69, translations mine. *Othello* apparently was being performed in Paris at around the same time (Everist, *Music Drama*, 55).

43. *London Literary Gazette*, 22 May 1824.

44. "Modes," *Le Diable boiteux*, 25 May 1824.

45. Ourika Mania precedes the American trope of blackface minstrelsy, which also did not include white women. See Lott, *Love and Theft*; Bean, *Inside the Minstrel Mask*; Toll, *Blacking Up*; Lhamon, *Raising Cain*.

46. *Le Corsaire*, 4 April 1824; and *Journal de Paris*, 13 May 1824, quoted in Chalaye, *Les Ourika du boulevard*, xxvii, translation mine.

47. Ibid., xxvii, translation mine.

48. Ourika was also the subject of at least one other poem, Ulric Guttinger's "Ourika, Romance" (1825) (Roger Little, introduction to Duras, *Ourika*, ed. Little, 98; Hoffmann, *Le Nègre romantique*, 226), as well as a novella, Dudon, *La Nouvelle Ourika*. In addition, painter François Pascal Simon Gérard rendered

her in 1823 on a Sèvres porcelain vase (now in the private collection of the Château d'Ussé in Indre-et-Loire, France), and Alfred Johannot created an etching depicting the same scene; its location is unknown.

49. Gay, "Ourika Élégie," 2–3; Schultz, *Anthology of Nineteenth-Century Women's Poetry*, trans. Rivers and Schultz, 66; Kale, *French Salons*, 103.
50. Sharpley-Whiting, "Black Blood," 55.
51. Pons, "Ourika, l'africaine," 220, translation mine.
52. Hoffmann, *Nègre romantique*, 225, translation mine.
53. Pons, "Ourika, l'africaine," 220, translation mine.
54. Vieillard, *Ourika, stances élégiaques*, translations mine.
55. *Journal du commerce*, 18, 30 April 1824, quoted in Davidson, *France after Revolution*, 159. According to Davidson, "Sufficient numbers of black men and women lived in France during the period to justify Napoleonic legislation creating a special surveillance apparatus for them." In fact, according to Peabody, *There Are No Slaves in France*, the number of blacks was disproportionate to the rhetoric about them.
56. Harms, *Diligent*, 16.
57. Davidson, *France after Revolution*, 159.
58. Ibid., 161.
59. According to Davidson, "In addition to confirming the widespread enthusiasm for the novel and its main character, the café Ourika's choice of employees demonstrates the prevalence of 'Orientalism,' as men rushed to enjoy the experience of being served by such exotic women" (ibid., 160). However, the specific link to Orientalism overlooks the prevalence of negrophobia and negrophilia in conjunction with Orientalism.
60. Bhabha, "Of Mimicry and Man," 153.

CHAPTER 4. JEANNE DUVAL

1. Flaubert, *Sentimental Education*, trans. Parmée, 7, 25–26.
2. Christophe, "Jeanne Duval," 428, 435. For Duval's same-sex relationships, see Aldrich and Wotherspoon, *Who's Who in Gay and Lesbian History*, 158; Gedo, *Psychoanalytic Perspectives on Art*, 2:72.
3. For works that devote significant attention to Duval, see Richon, *Jeanne Duval et Charles Baudelaire*; Rivers, "Black Venus"; Pichois, "A Propos d'un Poème de Baudelaire"; Pasinetti, "The 'Jeanne Duval' Poems"; Deguy, "Le Corps de Jeanne"; Ahearn, "Black Woman, White Poet"; Tonkin, "Musing on Baudelaire"; Henry, "Baudelaire's 'Chanson d'après-midi'"; Jacques Crépet, "Une Femme à enterrer," 149–55; Eugène Crépet, "Charles Baudelaire et

Jeanne Duval," *La Plume*, 15 April 1898; Beatrice Stith Clark, "Elements of Black Exoticisms," 63–65; Balakian, "Those Stigmatized Poems of Baudelaire"; Ferrier, "Histoire de Jeanne Duval."

4. Tillotson, "Materialist Feminist Reading of Jeanne Duval," 292.

5. Stoler, *Race and the Education of Desire*, 105.

6. Baudelaire to his stepfather, 8 December 1848, in Baudelaire, *Letters of Charles Baudelaire to His Mother*, trans. Symons, 34.

7. Baudelaire to his mother, 27 March 1852, in ibid., 43.

8. Ibid., 44–46.

9. Baudelaire to his mother, 26 March 1853, *Selected Letters of Charles Baudelaire*, trans. Lloyd, 57. See also Christophe, "Jeanne Duval," 434.

10. Baudelaire to his mother, 1854, quoted in Pichois, *Baudelaire*, trans. Robb, 210.

11. Baudelaire to his mother, 4 November 1856, in Baudelaire, *Letters of Charles Baudelaire to His Mother*, trans. Symons, 97.

12. Baudelaire to his mother, 1856, in Starkie, *Baudelaire*, 283.

13. "Gustave Courbet."

14. "Baudelaire and the Impressionist Revolution." This practice foreshadows the erasure of Russian figures from Soviet works during the 1930s. See King, *Commissar Vanishes*.

15. Pollock, *Differencing the Canon*, 264.

16. Fallaize, *Étienne Carjat and "Le Boulevard,"* 131.

17. Here I disagree with Pollock, who writes that "the figure assumed to be Jeanne Duval is represented in direct opposition to the demonised, exoticised, bestialised image produced by Baudelaire's contemporaries . . . and gives us, today's readers and viewers, relief in imagining another history than that given so repetitiously and maliciously in the canonical literature" (*Differencing the Canon*, 257–58). For a discussion of this controversy, see Dolan, "Skirting the Issue," 611.

18. Caroline Aupick to Charles Asselineau, 24 March 1868, in Crépet, *Crépet, and Asselineau, Baudelaire*, 267, translation mine.

19. Christophe, "Jeanne Duval," 428.

20. Charles Toubin quoted in Pichois, *Baudelaire*, trans. Robb, 204.

21. Banville, *Petites Études*, 74–75, translation mine.

22. Pollock, *Differencing the Canon*, 268.

23. Edmond Lepelletier, "La Statue de Baudelaire," *L'Echo de Paris*, 17 August 1892, translation mine.

24. Nadar, *Charles Baudelaire*, 7–8.

25. This continuing dismissal is one of the reasons so much more is known

about Apollonie Sabatier, a white woman with whom Baudelaire was briefly infatuated, than about Duval, his longtime companion. Unlike the Vénus Noire, the Vénus Blanche received the elevated status of courtesan. Yet Sabatier carried with her one of Baudelaire's drawings on which the infuriated woman had scrawled the words *his ideal* over Duval's face (Starkie, *Baudelaire*, 333–34). For more on Sabatier, see Senneville, *La Présidente*; Hoyle, "Changing Images of Madame Apollonie Sabatier"; Porché, *Baudelaire et la présidente*; Mermaz, *Madame Sabatier*; Théophile Gautier, *Lettre à la présidente*; Rounding, *Grandes horizontales*; Billy, *La Présidente et ses amis*; Moss, *Baudelaire et Madame Sabatier*.

26. See Richon, *Jeanne Duval et Charles Baudelaire*; Pichois, *Baudelaire*, trans. Robb.

27. In *Painting of Modern Life* (1984), art scholar T. J. Clark discusses the painting in minute detail but barely mentions the black maid who occupies half the painting. In subsequent editions of his book, Clark admits to being admonished by a colleague for this omission and offers a mea culpa. See T. J. Clark, *Painting of Modern Life* (1999), xxvii.

28. See, e.g., Crépet, "Une Femme à enterrer"; Hyslop and Hyslop, *Baudelaire: A Self-Portrait*.

29. Baudelaire, *Baudelaire: A Self Portrait*.

30. Reynold, *Charles Baudelaire*, 41, translation mine.

31. Porché, *Charles Baudelaire*, trans. Mavin, 70, 71.

32. Ibid., 70–71.

33. Ibid., 71–72.

34. Ibid., 72–73, 75, 79, 89.

35. Starkie, *Baudelaire*, 84, 85.

36. Ibid., 239, 394, 240.

37. Turnell, *Baudelaire*, 59–60.

38. Ibid., 60.

39. A. E. Carter, *Charles Baudelaire*, 37, 64, 38.

40. Ibid., 65, 70.

41. Hemmings, *Baudelaire the Damned*, 184.

42. Glyn, *Companion Guide to Paris*, 36.

43. Pichois, "A Propos des 'Yeux de Berthe' du nouveau sur Jeanne Duval?," 62n114, translation mine. Pichois's *Baudelaire: Études et témoignages* offers the most comprehensive account of Duval's life in the theater: Pichois painstakingly researched theater bulletins and reviews to find bit parts that she played.

44. Berlanstein, *Daughters of Eve*, 24, 40, 101, 103, 119.

45. Ibid., 116.
46. Stoler, *Race and the Education of Desire*, 105.
47. Ibid., 100.

CONCLUSION

1. Baker and Chase, *Josephine*, 5, 111.
2. Mills, *Racial Contract*, 86.
3. Baldwin, *Giovanni's Room*, 32.

BIBLIOGRAPHY

Abrahams, Yvette. "Images of Sara Baartmann: Sexuality, Race, and Gender in Early-Nineteenth-Century Britain." In *Nation, Empire, Colony: Historicizing Gender and Race*, ed. Ruth Roach Pierson and Nupur Chaudhuri. Bloomington: Indiana University Press, 1998.

"African Venus." Walters Art Museum, http://art.thewalters.org/detail/15324/african-venus/.

Ahearn, Edward J. "Black Woman, White Poet: Exile and Exploitation in Baudelaire's Jeanne Duval Poems." *French Review* 51 (December 1977): 212–20.

Albigès, Luce-Marie. "Portrait d'une négresse." *Histoire par l'image* (February 2007), http://www.histoire-image.org/etudes/portrait-negresse.

Aldrich, Robert, and Garry Wotherspoon. *Who's Who in Gay and Lesbian History: From Antiquity to World War II*. New York: Routledge, 2001.

Anderson, Benedict. *Imagined Communities: Reflections on the Origin and Spread of Nationalism*. London: Verso, 1991.

Austin, Paul Britten. *1815: The Return of Napoleon*. London: Greenhill, 2002.

Badou, Gérard. *L'Énigme de la Vénus hottentote*. Paris: Lattès, 2000.

Baker, Jean-Claude, and Chris Chase. *Josephine: The Hungry Heart*. New York: Random House, 1993.

Balakian, Anna. "Those Stigmatized Poems of Baudelaire." *French Review* 31, no. 4 (February 1958): 273–77.

Baldwin, James. *Giovanni's Room*. 1956. New York: Dell, 1984.

Banville, Théodore de. *Petites Études: Mes Souvenirs*. Paris: Charpentier, 1882.

Baudelaire, Charles. *Baudelaire: A Self Portrait: Selected Letters*. Trans. and ed. Lois Boe Hyslop and Francis E. Hyslop Jr. London: Oxford University Press, 1957.

———. *Correspondance générale*. Ed. Jacques Crépet. Paris: Conard, 1947.

———. *The Letters of Charles Baudelaire to His Mother, 1833–1866*. Trans. Arthur Symons. New York: Haskell House Publishers, Ltd., 1971.

———. *Lettres, 1841–1866*. Paris: Mercure de France, 1907.

———. *Œuvres complètes de Charles Baudelaire*. Ed. Jacques Crépet. Paris: Conard, 1953.

———. *Selected Letters of Charles Baudelaire: The Conquest of Solitude*. Trans. and ed. Rosemary Lloyd. Chicago: University of Chicago Press, 1986.

"Baudelaire and the Impressionist Revolution." http://impressionist1877.tripod.com/realism.htm.

Bean, Annemarie, ed. *Inside the Minstrel Mask: Readings in Nineteenth-Century Blackface Minstrelsy*. Hanover, N.H.: Wesleyan University Press, 1996.

Beauvau, Marie-Charlotte de. *Souvenirs de la maréchale princesse de Beauvau, née Rohan-Chabot, suivis des mémoires du Maréchal prince de Beauvau*. Paris: Techener, 1872.

Bell, David Avrom. *The Cult of the Nation in France: Inventing Nationalism, 1680–1800*. Cambridge: Harvard University Press, 2001.

Berlanstein, Lenard R. *Daughters of Eve: A Cultural History of French Theater Women from the Old Regime to the Fin de Siècle*. Cambridge: Harvard University Press, 2001.

[Bernier, François]. "Nouvelle Division de la terre par les différentes espèces ou races qui l'habitent." *Journal des sçavans* [savants], 24 April 1684.

Bertrand-Jennings, Chantal. "*Ourika* and Women's Literary Tradition in France." In *Approaches to Teaching Duras's Ourika*, ed. Mary Ellen Birkett and Christopher Rivers. New York: Modern Language Association, 2009.

Bhabha, Homi. "Of Mimicry and Man: The Ambivalence of Colonial Discourse." In *Tensions of Empire: Colonial Cultures in a Bourgeois World*, ed. Frederick Cooper and Ann Laura Stoler. Berkeley: University of California Press, 1997.

Billy, André. *La Présidente et ses amis*. Paris: Flammarion, 1945.

Bindman, David. *Ape to Apollo. Aesthetics and the Idea of Race in the Eighteenth Century*. Ithaca: Cornell University Press, 2002.

Birkett, Mary Ellen, and Christopher Rivers, eds. *Approaches to Teaching Duras's Ourika*. New York: Modern Language Association, 2009.

Blachère, Jean-Claude. *Le Modèle Nègre: Aspects littéraires du mythe primitiviste au XXe siècle chez Apollinaire, Cendrars, Tzara*. Dakar: Nouvelles Editions Africaines, 1981.

Blainville, Henri de. "Sur une Femme de la race hottentote." *Bulletin des sciences par la société philomatique de Paris* (1816): 183–90.

Blumenbach, Johann Friedrich. "The Degeneration of the Races." In *Race and the Enlightenment: A Reader*, ed. Emmanuel Chukwedi Eze. Cambridge: Blackwell, 1997.

Boom, Rori. "Monkey-Girls of Old Regime France: Babiole and Ourika." *Nottingham French Studies* 49, no. 1 (March 2010): 19–30.

Bonneserre de Saint-Denis, Émile. *Revue nobiliaire, héraldique, et biographique.* Vol. 9. Paris: Dumoulin, 1874.

Boré. *Faits relatifs aux troubles de Saint-Domingue.* Paris: Patriote Français, 1792.

Boulle, Pierre H. "François Bernier and the Origins of the Modern Concept of Race." In *The Color of Liberty: Histories of Race in France*, ed. Sue Peabody and Tyler Edward Stovall. Durham: Duke University Press, 2003.

———. *Race et esclavage dans la France de l'ancien régime.* Paris: Perrin, 2007.

Boulle, Pierre H., and Sue Peabody. *Le Droit des noirs en France au temps de l'esclavage: Textes choisis et commentés.* Paris: L'Harmattan, 2015.

Brady, Heather. "Recovering Claire de Duras's Creole Inheritance: Race and Gender in the Exile's Correspondence of Her Saint-Domingue Family." *L'Esprit créateur* 47, no. 4 (Winter 2007): 44–56.

Burrows, Simon. *French Exile: Journalism and European Politics, 1782–1814.* Suffolk: Royal Historical Society, 2001.

Calvé, Emma. *Sous Tous les Ciels j'ai chanté.* Paris: Plon, 1940.

Carter, A. E. *Charles Baudelaire.* Boston: Twayne, 1977.

Carter, Angela. *Black Venus's Tale.* London: Next Editions, 1980.

Chalaye, Sylvie. *Nègres en images.* Paris: L'Harmattan, 2002.

———. *Du Noir au nègre: L'Image du noir au théâtre, de Marguerite de Navarre à Jean Genet (1550–1960).* Paris: L'Harmattan, 1998.

———. *Les Ourikas du boulevard.* Paris: L'Harmattan, 2003.

Chapman, Herrick, and Laura Levine Frader. *Race in France: Interdisciplinary Perspectives on the Politics of Difference.* New York: Berghahn, 2004.

"Charles Baudelaire." *Poetry Foundation*, http://www.poetryfoundation.org/bio/charles-baudelaire.

Cheyne, Michelle. "Love No Other: Staging Race and Desire in French Restoration Drama." Paper presented at the International Nineteenth Century French Studies Colloquium: Empire, Identity, Exoticism, Vanderbilt University, Nashville, 18 October 2009.

Chilcoat, Michelle. "Civility, Marriage, and the Impossible French Citizen: From *Ourika* to *Zouzou* and *Princesse Tam Tam*." *Colby Quarterly* 37, no. 2 (June 2001): 125–44.

———. "Confinement, the Family Institution, and the Case of Claire de Duras' Ourika." *L'Esprit Créateur* 38, no. 3 (Fall 1998): 6–16.

Childs, Adrienne L. "The Black Exotic: Tradition and Ethnography in Nineteenth-Century Orientalist Art." PhD diss., University of Maryland, 2005.

Christophe, Marc-A. "Jeanne Duval: Baudelaire's Black Venus or Baudelaire's Demon?" *CLA Journal* 33, no. 4 (June 1990): 428–39.

Clare, Eli. *Exile and Pride: Disability, Queerness, and Liberation*. Cambridge: South End, 1999.

Clark, Beatrice Stith. "Elements of Black Exoticism in the 'Jeanne Duval' Poems of 'Les Fleurs du Mal.'" *Black Studies: International Dimensions* 14, no. 1 (September 1970): 62–74.

Clark, T. J. *The Painting of Modern Life: Paris in the Art of Manet and His Followers*. Princeton: Princeton University Press, 1984.

———. *The Painting of Modern Life: Paris in the Art of Manet and His Followers*. Rev. ed. Princeton: Princeton University Press, 1999.

Cobban, Alfred. *A History of Modern France*. Vol. 2, *From the First Empire to the Second Empire, 1799–1871*. London: Penguin, 1986.

Cocherel, Nicolas-Robert. *Observations de M. de Cocherel, . . . sur le mémoire du ministre de la marine*. Paris: Clousier, 1791.

Cohen, William B. *The French Encounter with Africans: White Response to Blacks, 1530–1880*. Bloomington: Indiana University Press, 2003.

Coller, Ian. *Arab France: Islam and the Making of Modern Europe, 1798–1831*. Berkeley: University of California Press, 2011.

Colnet du Ravel, Charles Joseph. "Sartjée; ou, La Vénus hottentote à son cousin." In *Mœurs françaises: L'Hermite du faubourg Saint-Germain; ou, Observations sur les mœurs et les usages français au commencement du XIXe siècle*. Paris: Pillet Ainé, 1825.

Cooper, Barbara T. "*Staging Ourika* and the Spectacle of Difference." In *Ethnography in French Literature*, ed. B. Norman. Amsterdam: Rodopi, 1996.

Cooper, Frederick, and Ann Laura Stoler. "Between Metropole and Colony: Towards a New Research Perspective." In *Tensions of Empire: Colonial Culture in a Bourgeois World*, ed. Frederick Cooper and Ann Laura Stoler. Berkeley: University of California Press, 1997.

Cowles, Jane. "The Subjectivity of the Colonial Subject from Olympe de Gouges to Mme de Duras." *L'Esprit créateur* 47, no. 4 (2007): 29–43.

Crais, Clifton C., and Pamela Scully. *Sara Baartman and the Hottentot Venus: A Ghost Story and a Biography*. Princeton: Princeton University Press, 2011.

Crépet, Eugène, Jacques Crépet, and Charles Asselineau. *Baudelaire: Étude biographique d'Eugène Crépet*. Paris: Messein, 1928.

Crépet, Jacques. "Une Femme à enterrer." In *Propos sur Baudelaire*, comp. and annot. Claude Pichois. Paris: Mercure de France, 1957.

Cresswell, Julia, ed. *The Oxford Dictionary of Word Origins*. Oxford: Oxford University Press, 2010.

Crofts, Marylee S. "Duras's Ourika: Race and Gender in Text and Context." PhD diss., University of Wisconsin at Madison, 1992.

"Curiosities and Exhibits." http://www.nationalarchives.gov.uk/pathways/blackhistory/culture/curiosities.htm.

Cuvier, Georges. "Extrait d'observations faites sur le cadavre d'une femme connue à Paris et à Londres sous le nom de Vénus hottentotte." *Mémoires du Muséum d'histoire naturelle* 3 (1817): 259–74.

―――. "The Race from Which We Are Descended Has Been Called Caucasian . . . the Handsomest on Earth." In *Race and the Enlightenment: A Reader*, ed. Emmanuel Chukwedi Eze. Cambridge: Blackwell, 1997.

Dalbello, Marij, and Mary Lewis Shaw. *Visible Writings: Cultures, Forms, Readings*. New Brunswick, N.J.: Rutgers University Press, 2011.

Daniels, Stephen, and Denis Cosgrove. "Introduction: Iconography and Landscape." In *Iconography of Landscapes: Essays on the Symbolic Representation, Design, and Use of Past Environments*, ed. Stephen Daniels, Denis Cosgrove, and Alan R. Baker. Cambridge: Cambridge University Press, 1988.

Darnton, Robert. "An Early Information Society: News and the Media in Eighteenth-Century Paris." *American Historical Review* 105, no. 1 (February 2000): 1–35.

Davidson, Denise Z. *France after Revolution: Urban Life, Gender, and the New Social Order*. Cambridge: Harvard University Press, 2007.

Davis, Lennard. *Bending over Backwards: Disability, Dismodernism and Other Difficult Positions*. New York: New York University Press, 2002.

―――, ed. *The Disability Studies Reader*. New York: Routledge, 2017.

―――. *Enforcing Normalcy: Disability, Deafness, and the Body*. London: Verso, 1995.

Debrunner, Hans. *Presence and Prestige, Africans in Europe: A History of Africans in Europe before 1918*. Basel: Basler Afrika Bibliographien, 1979.

De Groot, Joanna. "'Sex' and 'Race': The Construction of Language and Image in the Nineteenth Century." In *Sexuality and Subordination: Interdisciplinary Studies of Gender in the Nineteenth Century*, ed. Susan Mendus and Jane Rendall. New York: Routledge, 1989.

Deguy, Michel. "Le Corps de Jeanne." *Poetique* 3 (1970): 334–47.

De Raedt, Thérèse. "Ourika: L'Inspiration de Mme. de Duras." *Dalhousie French Studies* 73 (Winter 2005): 19–33.

———. "Ourika en noir et blanc: Une Femme africaine en France." PhD diss., University of California at Davis, 2000.

———. "Ourika in Black and White: Textual and Visual Interplay." *Women in French Studies* 12 (2004): 45–69.

———. "Representations of the Real-Life Ourika." In *Approaches to Teaching Duras's Ourika*, ed. Mary Ellen Birkett and Christopher Rivers. New York: Modern Language Association, 2009.

de Vaux de Foletier, F. "Sources d'histoire coloniale aux Archives de la Seine." *Revue d'histoire des colonies* 38, no. 135 (1951): 359–66.

DiMauro, Damon. "*Ourika*; or, Galatea Reverts to Stone." *Nineteenth-Century French Studies* 28, nos. 3–4 (Spring–Summer 2000): 187–211.

Dobie, Madeleine. *Trading Places: Colonization and Slavery in Eighteenth-Century French Culture*. Ithaca: Cornell University Press, 2010.

Dolan, Therese. "Skirting the Issue: Manet's Portrait of Baudelaire's Mistress, Reclining." *Art Bulletin* 79, no. 4 (December 1997): 611–29.

Doy, Gen. "More Than Meets the Eye: Representations of Black Women in Mid-19th-Century French Photography." *Women's Studies International Forum* 21, no. 3 (May 1998): 305–19.

Dudon, Mme. M.-A. *La Nouvelle Ourika; ou, Les Avantages de l'éducation*. Paris, 1824.

Duras, Claire de Durfort, Duchesse de. *Ourika*. Trans. John Fowles, intro. Joan DeJean and Margaret Waller. New York: Modern Language Association of America, 1994.

———. *Ourika*. Ed. Roger Little. Exeter: University of Exeter Press, 1998.

Eichthal, Gustave d', and Ismayl Urbain. *Lettres sur la race noire et la race blanche*. Paris: Paulin, 1839.

Eliel, Carol S. "Louis-Léopold Boilly's 'The Galleries of the Palais-Royal.'" *Burlington Magazine* 126, no. 974 (May 1984): 269–70, 275–276, 279.

Everist, Mark. *Music Drama at the Paris Odéon, 1824–1828*. Berkeley: University of California Press, 2002.

Ezra, Elizabeth. *The Colonial Unconscious: Race and Culture in Interwar France*. Ithaca: Cornell University Press, 2000.

"Facing the Other: Charles Cordier (1827–1905), Ethnographic Sculptor." *Musée d'Orsay*, http://www.musee-orsay.fr/en/events/exhibitions/archives/exhibitions-archives/browse/14/article/charles-cordier-1827-1905-sculpteur-lautre-et-lailleurs-4210.html?S=&tx_ttnews[backPid]=252&cHash=15b9e8ec62&print=1&no_cache=1&.

Fallaize, Elizabeth. *Étienne Carjat and "Le Boulevard" (1861–1863)*. Geneva: Slatkine, 1987.

Fanoudh-Seifer, Léon. *Le Mythe du nègre et de l'Afrique noire dans la littérature française de 1800 à la deuxième guerre mondiale*. Paris: Klincksieck, 1968.

Fausto-Sterling, Anne. "Gender, Race, and Nation: The Comparative Anatomy of 'Hottentot' Women in Europe: 1815–1817." In *Deviant Bodies: Critical Perspectives on Difference in Science and Popular Culture*, ed. Jennifer Terry and Jacqueline Urla. Bloomington: Indiana University Press, 1995.

Fauvelle-Aymar, Francois-Xavier. *L'Invention du hottentot: Histoire du regard occidental sur les Khoisan, XVe–XIXe siècle*. Paris: Publications de la Sorbonne, 2002.

Fay, Carolyn. "He Said, She Said: *Ourika* in a Gender Studies Course." In *Approaches to Teaching Duras's Ourika*, ed. Mary Ellen Birkett and Christopher Rivers. New York: Modern Language Association, 2009.

Ferrier, Michaël. "Histoire de Jeanne Duval, la 'Belle d'Abandon.'" In *Sympathie pour le fantôme*. Paris: Gallimard, 2010.

Fields, Jill. *An Intimate Affair: Women, Lingerie, and Sexuality*. Berkeley: University of California Press, 2007.

Flaubert, Gustave. *A Sentimental Education: The Story of a Young Man*. Oxford: Oxford University Press, 2000.

Fogarty, Richard Standish. *Race and War in France: Colonial Subjects in the French Army, 1914–1918*. Baltimore: Johns Hopkins University Press, 2008.

Fuentes, Marisa J. *Dispossessed Lives: Enslaved Women, Violence, and the Archive*. Philadelphia: University of Pennsylvania Press, 2016.

Garran de Coulon, Jean-Philippe. *Rapport sur les troubles de Saint-Domingue*. Paris: Imprimerie Nationale, 1797.

Garraway, Doris. *The Libertine Colony: Creolization in the Early French Caribbean*. Durham: Duke University Press, 2005.

Gautier, Arlette. *Les Sœurs de solitude: La Condition féminine dans l'esclavage aux Antilles du XVIIe au XIXe siècle*. Paris: Caribéennes, 1985.

Gautier, Théophile. *Lettre à la présidente*. Monaco: Sauret, 1993.

Gay, Delphine. "Ourika Élégie." In *An Anthology of Nineteenth-Century Women's Poetry from France*, ed. Gretchen Schultz, trans. Anne Atik et al. New York: Modern Language Association, 2008.

Gedo, Mary Mathews. *Psychoanalytic Perspectives on Art: PPA*. Hillsdale, N.J.: Analytic, 1987.

Gheusi, Pierre-Barthelémy. *Cinquante Ans de Paris*. Paris: Plon, 1940.

Ghosh, Durba. *Sex and the Family in Colonial India: The Making of Empire*. Cambridge: Cambridge University Press, 2006.

Gildea, Robert. *Children of the Revolution: The French, 1799–1914*. Cambridge: Harvard University Press, 2008.

Gilman, Sander L. "Black Bodies, White Bodies: Toward an Iconography of Female Sexuality in Late Nineteenth-Century Art, Medicine, and Literature." *Critical Inquiry* 12, no. 1 (Autumn 1985): 204–42.

———. "Black Bodies, White Bodies: Toward an Iconography of Female Sexuality in Late Nineteenth-Century Art, Medicine, and Literature." In *"Race," Writing, and Difference*, ed. Henry Louis Gates Jr. Chicago: University of Chicago Press, 1986.

———. "Black Sexuality and Modern Consciousness." In *Blacks and German Culture*, ed. Reinhold Grimm and Jost Hermand. Madison: University of Wisconsin Press, 1986.

———. *Difference and Pathology: Stereotypes of Sexuality, Race, and Madness*. Ithaca: Cornell University Press, 1985.

Gilroy, Paul. *The Black Atlantic: Modernity and Double Consciousness*. Cambridge: Harvard University Press, 1993.

Glyn, Anthony. *The Companion Guide to Paris*. Rev. Susan Glyn. Woodbridge: Companion Guides, 2000.

Grigsby, Darcy Grimaldo. *Extremities: Painting Empire in Post-Revolutionary France*. New Haven: Yale University Press, 2002.

———. "Revolutionary Sons, White Fathers, and Creole Difference: Guillaume Guillon-Lethière's 'Oath of the Ancestors' (1822)." *Yale French Studies* 101 (2001): 201–26.

"Gustave Courbet: *The Artist's Studio*." Musée d'Orsay, http://www.musee-orsay.fr/index.php?id=851&L=1&tx_commentaire_pi1%5BshowUid%5D=7091.

Hargreaves, Alec G. *Immigration, "Race," and Ethnicity in Contemporary France*. London: Routledge, 1995.

Harms, Robert W. *The Diligent: A Voyage through the Worlds of the Slave Trade*. New York: Basic Books, 2003.

Hemmings, Frederick William John. *Baudelaire the Damned: A Biography*. New York: Scribner's, 1982.

Henry, Freeman G. "Baudelaire's 'Chanson d'après-midi' and the Return of Jeanne Duval." *Kentucky Romance Quarterly* 24 (1977): 95–107.

Hesse, Carla. *The Other Enlightenment: How French Women Became Modern*. Princeton: Princeton University Press, 2010.

Heuer, Jennifer Ngaire. *The Family and the Nation: Gender and Citizenship in Revolutionary France, 1789–1830*. Ithaca: Cornell University Press, 2007.

Higginbotham, Evelyn Brooks. "African-American Women's History and the Metalanguage of Race." *Signs* 17, no. 2 (Winter 1992): 251–74.

Hobsbawm, Eric J. *Nations and Nationalism since 1780: Programme, Myth, Reality*. Cambridge: Cambridge University Press, 1990.

Hoffmann, Léon-François. *Le Nègre romantique: Personnage littéraire et obsession collective*. Paris: Payot, 1973.

Holmes, Rachel. *African Queen: The Real Life of the Hottentot Venus*. New York: Random House, 2007.

Honour, Hugh, and John Fleming. *A World History of Art*. London: King, 2014.

Hopkinson, Nalo. *The Salt Roads*. New York: Warner, 2003.

Howland, John. *The Letter Form and the French Enlightenment: The Epistolary Paradox*. New York: Lang, 1991.

Hoyle, Marie Heather. "The Changing Images of Madame Apollonie Sabatier: Emblems of Sexualité, Égalité, Fidélité, and Fraternité." Master's thesis, Michigan State University, 2004.

Hunt, Lynn. *The Family Romance of the French Revolution*. Berkeley: University of California Press, 1992.

Ingersoll, Earl G. "The Appropriation of Black Experience in the *Ourika* of Claire de Duras." *CEA Critic* 60 (Spring–Summer 1998): 1–13.

Jennings, Lawrence. *French Anti-Slavery: The Movement for the Abolition of Slavery in France, 1802–1848*. Cambridge: Cambridge University Press, 2006.

———. *French Reaction to British Slave Emancipation*. Baton Rouge: Louisiana State University Press, 1988.

Jenson, Deborah. "Mirror Insurrections: Haitian and French Revolutions in *Ourika*." In *Approaches to Teaching Duras's Ourika*, ed. Mary Ellen Birkett and Christopher Rivers. New York: Modern Language Association, 2009.

Kadish, Doris Y., and Françoise Massardier-Kenney, eds. *Translating Slavery: Gender and Race in French Women's Writing, 1783–1823*. Kent, Ohio: Kent State University Press, 1994.

———. *Translating Slavery*. 2nd ed. Kent, Ohio: Kent State University Press, 2010.

Kafer, Alison. "Desire and Disgust: My Ambivalent Adventures in Devoteeism." In *Sex and Disability*, ed. Robert McRuer and Anna Mollow. Durham: Duke University Press, 2012.

———. *Feminist, Queer, Crip*. Bloomington: Indiana University Press, 2013.

Kale, Steven. *French Salons: High Society and Political Sociability from the Old Regime to the Revolution of 1848*. Baltimore: Johns Hopkins University Press, 2004.

Kelly, Dorothy. "*Ourika* and the Reproduction of Social Forms: Duras and

Bourdieu." In *Approaches to Teaching Duras's Ourika*, ed. Mary Ellen Birkett and Christopher Rivers. New York: Modern Language Association, 2009.

King, David. *The Commissar Vanishes: The Falsification of Photographs and Art in Stalin's Russia*. New York: Metropolitan/Holt, 1997.

Kirby, Percival. "The Hottentot Venus." *Africana Notes and News* 6, no. 3 (1949): 55–62.

———. "More about the Hottentot Venus." *Africana Notes and News* 10, no. 4 (1953): 124–34.

Kroen, Sheryl. *Politics and Theater: The Crisis of Legitimacy in Restoration France, 1815–1830*. Berkeley: University of California Press, 2000.

Kumar, Krishan. "English and French National Identity: Comparisons and Contrasts." *Nations and Nationalism* 12, no. 3 (July 2006): 413–32.

Kwon, Yun Kyong. "'Remember Saint Domingue': Accounts of the Haitian Revolution by Refugee Planters in Paris and Colonial Debates under the Restoration, 1814–1825." In *France's Lost Empires: Fragmentation, Nostalgia, and la Fracture Coloniale*, ed. Kate Marsh and Nicola Frith. Lanham, Md.: Lexington Books, 2011.

Lafont, Anne. "Madeline." In *Le Modèle noire: De Géricault à Matisse*. Paris: Museé d'Orsay/Flammarion, 2019.

Larchevesque-Thibaud. *Notes sur les troubles de Saint-Domingue*. Paris: Testu, 1793.

La Tour du Pin, Henriette Lucie Dillon. *Journal d'une femme de cinquante ans (1778–1815)*. Volume 1. Paris: Librairie Chapelot, 1913.

Lévy, Marianne. *Marie-Guillemine Laville-Leroulx et les siens: Une Femme peintre de l'ancien régime à la restauration (1768–1826)*. Paris: L'Harmattan, 2018.

Lhamon, W. T. *Raising Cain: Blackface Performance from Jim Crow to Hip Hop*. Cambridge: Harvard University Press, 1998.

Lindfors, Bernth. "Ethnological Show Business: Footlighting the Dark Continent." In *Freakery: Cultural Spectacles of the Extraordinary Body*, ed. Rosemarie Garland Thomson. New York: New York University Press, 1996.

———. "'The Hottentot Venus' and Other African Attractions in Nineteenth-Century England." *Australasian Drama Studies* 1, no. 2 (1983): 83–104.

Little, Roger. "Peau noire, masque blanc." In Claire de Durfort, duchesse de Duras, *Ourika*, ed. Roger Little. Exeter: University of Exeter Press, 1998.

———. "Le Nom et les origines d'Ourika." *Revue d'histoire littéraire de la France* 98, no. 4 (July–August 1998): 633–37.

Lott, Eric. *Love and Theft: Blackface Minstrelsy and the American Working Class*. New York: Oxford University Press, 1993.

Lowe, Kate. "The Stereotyping of Black Africans in Renaissance Europe." In *Black Africans in Renaissance Europe*, ed. T. F. Earle and K. J. P. Lowe. Cambridge: Cambridge University Press, 2005.

Martin, Emily. *Bipolar Expeditions: Mania and Depression in American Culture*. Princeton: Princeton University Press, 2009.

Maseko, Zola, dir. *The Life and Times of Sarah Baartmann*. Icarus Films, 1999.

Mathews, Mrs. Charles [Anne]. *Memoirs of Charles Mathews, Comedian*. London: Richard Bentley, 1839.

Maugras, Gaston, and Pierre de Croze-Lemercier. *Delphine de Sabran, Marquise de Custine*. Paris: Plon-Nourrit, 1912.

McClintock, Anne. *Imperial Leather: Race, Gender, and Sexuality in Colonial Context*. New York: Routledge, 1995.

McCloy, Shelby T. *The Negro in France*. Lexington: University of Kentucky Press, 1961.

Meadows, Darrell. "The Planters of Saint-Domingue, 1750–1804: Migration and Exile in the French Revolutionary Atlantic." PhD diss., Carnegie Mellon University, 2004.

Memmi, Albert. *The Colonizer and the Colonized*. Trans. Howard Greenfeld. New York: Orion, 1965.

Mermaz, Louis. *Madame Sabatier: Apollonie au pays des libertins*. Lausanne: Rencontre, 1967.

Merton, Tobias, ed. *The Literary Magnet of the Belles Lettres, Science, and the Fine Arts*. London, 1824.

Mignogna, Kim. "Ourika; ou, L'Échec des Lumières." In "L'Étrangère dans la société parisienne chez l'Abbé Prévost, Mme. de Graffigny, et Mme. de Duras." Master's thesis, University of Montreal, 2002.

Miller, Christopher L. *The French Atlantic Triangle: Literature and Culture of the Slave Trade*. Durham: Duke University Press, 2008.

Mills, Charles W. *The Racial Contract*. Ithaca: Cornell University Press, 1997.

Milscent, Claude. *Sur les Troubles de Saint-Domingue*. Paris: Patriote François, 1791.

Moitt, Bernard. *Women and Slavery in the French Antilles, 1635–1848*. Bloomington: Indiana University Press, 2001.

Montesquieu. *Lettres persanes*. Cologne: Marteau, 1721.

Montesquieu Charles de Secondat, Margaret Mauldon, and Andrew Kahn. *Persian Letters*. Oxford: Oxford University Press, 2008.

Morrison, Toni. "The Site of Memory." In *Inventing the Truth: The Art and Craft of Memoir*, ed. William Zinsser. Boston: Houghton Mifflin, 1995.

Moss, Armand. *Baudelaire et Madame Sabatier*. Paris: Nizet, 1978.

Mosse, George L. *Toward the Final Solution: A History of European Racism*. New York: Fertig, 1978.

Munford, Rebecca. "Re-Presenting Charles Baudelaire/Re-Presenting Jeanne Duval: Transformations of the Muse in Angela Carter's 'Black Venus.'" *Forum for Modern Language Studies* 40, no. 1 (2004): 1–13.

Nadar [Félix Tournachon, pseud.]. *Charles Baudelaire, intime, le poète vierge*. Paris: Blaizot, 1911.

Noiriel, Gérard. "National Identity, Nationality, and Citizenship." In *The French Melting Pot: Immigration, Citizenship, and National Identity*. Minneapolis: University of Minnesota Press, 1996.

O'Connell, David. "*Ourika*: Black Face, White Mask." *French Review* 47, no. 6 (Spring 1974): 47–56.

Page, Pierre-François. *Développement des causes des troubles et désastres des colonies françaises*. Paris: La Convention Nationale, 1793.

Palmer, Jennifer L. *Intimate Bonds: Family and Slavery in the French Atlantic*. Philadelphia: University of Pennsylvania Press, 2016.

Pasinetti, P. M. "The 'Jeanne Duval' Poems in Les Fleurs du Mal." *Yale French Studies* 2 (1948): 112–18.

Peabody, Sue. "'A Nation Born to Slavery': Missionaries and Racial Discourse in Seventeenth-Century French Antilles." *Journal of Social History* 38, no. 1 (Fall 2004): 113–26.

———. "Ourika in the History Classroom." In *Approaches to Teaching Duras's Ourika*, ed. Mary Ellen Birkett and Christopher Rivers. New York: Modern Language Association, 2009.

———. *There Are No Slaves in France: The Political Culture of Race and Slavery in the Ancien Régime*. New York: Oxford University Press, 1996.

Peabody, Sue, and Tyler Edward Stovall. *The Color of Liberty: Histories of Race in France*. Durham: Duke University Press, 2003.

Perry, George. *Ourika, the Orphan of Senegal; a Petite Drama, in One Act, with Songs, Translated from the French by Joseph Ebsworth*. Edinburgh: Ebsworth, 1828.

Pichois, Claude. "A Propos des 'Yeux de Berthe' du nouveau sur Jeanne Duval?" In *Baudelaire: Études et témoignages*. Neuchâtel: La Baconnière, 1967.

———. "A Propos d'un Poème de Baudelaire: Du Nouveau sur Jeanne Duval." *Revue d'histoire littéraire de la France* 55 (1955): 191–205.

———. *Baudelaire*. Trans. Graham Robb. London: Hamilton, 1989.

———. *Baudelaire: Études et témoignages*. Neuchâtel: La Baconnière, 1967.

Pieterse, Jan Nederveen. *White on Black: Images of Africa and Blacks in Western Popular Culture*. New Haven: Yale University Press, 1992.

Pollock, Griselda. *Differencing the Canon: Feminist Desire and the Writing of Art's Histories*. London: Routledge, 2006.

Pons, Gaspard de. "Ourika, l'africaine." In *Inspirations poétiques*. Paris: Urbain Canel, 1825.

Poole, Deborah. *Vision, Race, and Modernity: A Visual Economy of the Andean Image*. Princeton: Princeton University Press, 1997.

Popkin, Jeremy D. *Facing Racial Revolution: Eyewitness Accounts of the Haitian Insurrection*. Chicago: University of Chicago Press, 2007.

Porché, François. *Baudelaire et la Présidente*. Geneva: Milieu du Monde, 1941.

———. *Charles Baudelaire*. Trans. John Mavin. New York: Liveright, 1928.

Prasad, Pratima. *Colonialism, Race, and the French Romantic Imagination*. New York: Routledge, 2009.

Racine, Jean. *Britannicus*. Paris: Bélin, 1787.

Ransom, Amy J. "Mademoiselle Aïssé: Inspiration for Claire de Duras's *Ourika*?" *Romance Quarterly* 46, no. 2 (1999): 84–98.

Raymond [Raimond], Julien. *Réflexions sur les véritables causes des troubles et des désastres de nos colonies*. Paris: Patriotes, 1793.

Rétif de la Bretonne, N. E. *Le Palais-Royal: Première partie*. Paris, 1790.

Reynold, Gonzague de. *Charles Baudelaire*. Paris: Cres, 1920.

Richon, Emmanuel. *Jeanne Duval et Charles Baudelaire: Belle d'abandon*. Paris: L'Harmattan, 1999.

Rivers, W. Napoleon. "Black Venus—Jeanne Duval and Baudelaire's Sonnets." *Opportunity: Journal of Negro Life* 14, no. 1 (January 1936): 13–15.

Romanowski, Sylvie. *Through Strangers' Eyes: Fictional Foreigners in Old Regime France*. West Lafayette, Ind.: Purdue University Press, 2005.

Rouillard, Linda Marie. "The Black Galatea: Claire de Duras's *Ourika*." *Nineteenth-Century French Studies* 32, nos. 3–4 (Spring–Summer 2004): 207–22.

Rounding, Virginia. *Grandes Horizontales: The Lives and Legends of Marie Duplessis, Cora Pearl, La Païva, and La Présidente*. London: Bloomsbury, 2003.

Rushforth, Brett. *Bonds of Alliance: Indigenous and Atlantic Slaveries in New France*. Chapel Hill: University of North Carolina Press, 2014.

Sabran, Eléonore, and Stanislas-Jean de Boufflers. *La Comtesse de Sabran et le Chevalier de Boufflers: La Promesse, correspondance, 1786–1787*. Edited by Sue Carrell. Paris: Tallandier, 2010.

Said, Edward W. *Orientalism*. New York: Vintage, 1979.

Sandrel, Carole. *Vénus et hottentote: Sarah Bartman*. Paris: Perrin, 2010.
Schalk, Sami. "Coming to Claim Crip: Disidentification with/in Disability Studies." *Disability Studies Quarterly* 33, no. 2 (2013). http://dsq-sds.org/article/view/3705/3240.

———. "Metaphorically Speaking: Disability Metaphors in Feminist Writing." *Disability Studies Quarterly* 33, no. 4 (2013). http://dsq-sds.org/article/view/3874/3410.

Schechter, Ronald. *Obstinate Hebrews: Representations of Jews in France, 1715–1815*. Berkeley: University of California Press, 2003.

Schiebinger, Londa. "Skeletons in the Closet: The First Illustrations of the Female Skeleton in Eighteenth-Century Anatomy." In *The Making of the Modern Body: Sexuality and Society in the Nineteenth Century*, ed. Catherine Gallagher and Thomas Laqueur. Berkeley: University of California Press, 1987.

Schultz, Gretchen, ed. *An Anthology of Nineteenth-Century Women's Poetry from France*. Trans. Anne Atik et al. New York: Modern Language Association, 2008.

Seigel, Jerrold. *Bohemian Paris: Culture, Politics, and the Boundaries of Bourgeois Life*. Baltimore: Johns Hopkins University Press, 1999.

Senneville, Gérard de. *La Présidente: Une Égérie au XIXe siècle*. Paris: Stock, 1998.

Sepinwall, Alyssa Goldstein. "The Specter of Saint-Domingue: American and French Reactions to the Haitian Revolution." In *The World of the Haitian Revolution*, ed. Norman Fiering and David Geggus. Bloomington: Indiana University Press, 2009.

Sessions, Jennifer. *By Sword and Plow: France and the Conquest of Algeria*. Ithaca: Cornell University Press, 2016.

Sharpley-Whiting, T. Denean. "Black Blood, White Masks, and Négresse Sexuality in de Pons's *Ourika, l'africaine*." In *Black Venus: Sexualized Savages, Primal Fears, and Primitive Narratives in French*. Durham: Duke University Press, 1999.

———. *Black Venus: Sexualized Savages, Primal Fears, and Primitive Narratives in French*. Durham: Duke University Press, 1999.

———. "The Dawning of Racial-Sexual Science: A One Woman Showing, a One Man Telling, Sarah and Cuvier." In *Ethnography in French Literature*, ed. B. Norman. Amsterdam: Rodopi, 1996.

Silverstein, Paul A. *Algeria in France: Transpolitics, Race, and Nation*. Bloomington: Indiana University Press, 2004.

Smalls, James. "Exquisite Empty Shells: Sculpted Slave Portraits and the French

Ethnographic Turn." In *Slave Portraiture in the Atlantic World*, ed. Agnes Lugo-Ortiz and Angela Rosenthal. Cambridge: Cambridge University Press, 2016.

———. "Slavery Is a Woman: 'Race,' Gender, and Visuality in Marie Benoist's *Portrait d'une négresse* (1800)." *Nineteenth-Century Art Worldwide: A Journal of Nineteenth-Century Visual Culture* 3, no. 1 (Spring 2004). http://www.19thc-artworldwide.org/spring04index?id=178.

Sollors, Werner. *Neither Black nor White yet Both: Thematic Explorations of Interracial Literature*. Cambridge: Harvard University Press, 1997.

Solly, Samuel, and John George Moojen. "The Following Is the Result of the Examination of the Hottentot Venus—27th Nov. 1810." In *Africans on Stage: Studies in Ethnological Show Business*, ed. Bernth Lindfors. Bloomington: Indiana University Press, 1999.

Starkie, Enid. *Baudelaire*. New York: New Directions, 1958.

Stewart, John Hall. *The Restoration Era in France, 1814–1830*. Princeton, N.J.: Van Nostrand, 1968.

Stoler, Ann. *Race and the Education of Desire*. Durham: Duke University Press, 1995.

Stovall, Tyler, and Georges Van den Abbeele, eds. *French Civilization and Its Discontents: Nationalism, Colonialism, Race*. Lanham, Md.: Lexington Books, 2003.

Strother, Z. S. "Display of the Body Hottentot." In *Africans on Stage: Studies in Ethnological Show Business*, ed. Bernth Lindfors. Bloomington: Indiana University Press, 1999.

Tanner, James Mourilyan. *A History of the Study of Human Growth*. Cambridge: Cambridge University Press, 1981.

Taormina, Michael. "*L'Ourika* de Claire de Duras: Allégorie révolutionnaire, allégorie de la révolution." In *L'Afrique du siècle des Lumières: Savoirs et représentations*. Oxford: Voltaire Foundation, University of Oxford, 2009.

Théaulon, Marie-Emmanuel-Guillaume-Marguerite, Armand Dartois, and Nicolas Brasier. *La Vénus hottentote; ou, Haine aux françaises: Vaudeville en un acte*. Paris: Martinet, 1814.

Tillotson, Victoria P. "A Materialist Feminist Reading of Jeanne Duval: Prostitution and Sexual Imperialism from the Mid-Nineteenth Century to the Present Day." In *Materialist Feminism: A Reader in Class, Difference, and Women's Lives*, ed. Rosemary Hennessy and Chrys Ingraham. New York: Routledge, 1997.

Toll, Robert C. *Blacking Up: The Minstrel Show in Nineteenth-Century America*. London: Oxford University Press, 1974.

Tonkin, Maggie. "Musing on Baudelaire: Angela Carter's 'Black Venus' and the Poet as Dead Beloved." *Lit: Literature Interpretation Theory* 17, nos. 3–4 (July 2006): 301–23.

Tuori, Katri. "La Femme déracinée chez Claire de Duras et Gisèle Pineau." Unpublished paper, San Francisco State University, 2003.

Turnell, Martin. *Baudelaire: A Study of His Poetry*. New York: New Directions, 1972.

Vieillard, Pierre-Ange. *Ourika, stances élégiaques*. Paris: Pillet Aîné, 1824.

Warburton, Eileen. "Ashes, Ashes, We All Fall Down: Ourika, Cinderella, and the French Lieutenant's Woman." *Twentieth Century Literature* 42, no. 1 (Spring 1996): 165–86.

Weissmann, Gerald. *Darwin's Audubon: Science and the Liberal Imagination*. Cambridge: Perseus, 1998.

"Why Do the French Call the British 'the Roast Beefs'?" 3 April 2003, *BBC News*, http://news.bbc.co.uk/2/hi/2913151.stm.

Wilson, Elizabeth. *Bohemians: The Glamorous Outcasts*. New Brunswick, N.J.: Rutgers University Press, 2000.

Wiss, Rosemary. "Lipreading: Remembering Saartjie Baartman." *Australian Journal of Anthropology* 5, no. 3 (May 1994): 11–40.

Woolf, Virginia. *To the Lighthouse*. London: Hogarth, 1932.

Woshinsky, Barbara. "Teachings of *Ourika*." In *Approaches to Teaching Duras's Ourika*, ed. Mary Ellen Birkett and Christopher Rivers. New York: Modern Language Association, 2009.

INDEX

Page numbers in *italics* refer to illustrations

abolitionism: in England, 33–34; in France, 7, 19, 33, 55, 58, 109; Napoleon III's abolition of slavery, 109; Napoleon Bonaparte's reestablishment of slavery, 55; *Ourika* (Duras) and, 88

Baartmann, Sarah, xiii–xv, 14–15, 16, 17, 21, 84, 101, 102, 108, 109, 138, 140, 144n4, 147n29, 147n33, 148n38, 148n39; abolitionists and, 147n31; baptism, 34; baptismal certificate, 34, *35*, 148n38; birthplace of, 30, 146n26; and blackness, 79; body cast of, xiv, 38, *39*, *52*, 71; body of as scientific artifact, 54, 139; as challenge to ideas about Frenchness, 54, 57, 59, 61, 70, 138; contract to perform domestic duties and be exhibited, 30, 147n29; death of, 34, 38, 148n39; exhibitions of, 30–34; as fetish, 50; fragmentary information about, 49; Frenchness of, 138; and gender, 56, 57, 59, 79, 140; genitals of, 38–41, 72, 74; as "Hottentot Venus," 15, 30, *31*, 32, 33, 36, 38, 56, 57, 68–71, 72, 78; hypervisuality of, 108; as icon, 21; legal status of, 33–34, 147n29, 147n31; literary depictions of, 14, 56–57, 59–64, 68–71, 87, 91, 93; and miscegenation, 75; name of, 34, 144n37; as racial and cultural commodity, 49, 50, 54, 56, 140; and racial ventriloquism, 109; response of Londoners to, 30–32; response of Parisians to, 56–57; as scientific specimen, 38; sexualized representations of, 36, 56, 72, *73*, 74–75, 146n26; as symbol of uncivilized behavior, 72, 74, 78–79; time in England, 30, 31–34, 70, 148n38; time in Paris, 34, 36, 56, 59, 60, 65, 70; *La Vénus hottentote*, 59, 64–68, 93; visual depictions of, 71–78, *73*. *See also* colonial fantasies; racial ventriloquism

Baker, Josephine, 16, 135–37, *136*, 140

Baldwin, James, 135, 140

Balzac, Honoré de, 43

Banville, Théodore de, 43, 122

Baudelaire, Charles, 14, 16, 42, 44, 48, 117, 122, 123, 124, 139, 150n59, 150n64, 158n25; Apollonie Sabatier, relationship with, 158n25; biographers of, 16, 45, 107–9, 112, 124–33; bohemian lifestyle of, 110, 122; drawings of Jeanne Duval, 112, *113–16*; *Les Fleurs du mal*, 42, 107; handwriting style, 149n57; ideas about Frenchness, 109; portrayal of Jeanne Duval in writing, 42–43, 45–47, 107–8, 110–12; suicide attempt of, 45; visual depictions of, *106*, 117–20, *118*, *119*, 150n71

Beauvau, Maréchal Prince de, 15, 22, 24, 28

Beauvau, Marie-Charlotte de, 24, 26, 28–29

Benoist, Marie-Guillemine, 7–9, 142n17; *Portrait d'une négresse*, 7, 8, 9, 142n19
Berlanstein, Lenard R., 44, 131
Bhabha, Homi, 102
blackface, 95–96, 103; blackface minstrelsy, 156n45
blackness: as commodity, 49, 81, 92–93, 100; connection to colonies, 99; European debates about, 37; French imagination and, 12, 13, 70, 79, 86–87, 90, 100, 102, 109, 120; as impediment to romance, 96–99; markers of, 7, 54; as means to elevate whiteness, 96, 107; sexual attraction to, 66, 83; social constructions of, 11, 75. *See also* colonial fantasies; Haitian Revolution; miscegenation; "Ourika Mania"
blacks: in French missionary accounts, 3; as "house pets," 23; as inferior to whites, 36, 41; "masquerading" as whites, 95–96; representations of, eighteenth- and nineteenth-century, 4, 9–10; as symbols for socio-political positioning of whites, 4. *See also* colonial fantasies; racial drag; racial mimicry; racial ventriloquism
black women: African vs. French beauty trope, 69; bodies of, 3, 15, 32, 36, 38, 41, 83, 103; cultural representations of, 3, 6, 9, 11–14, 19; eroticization and hypersexualization of, 7, 9, 15, 38, 40, 66, 78, 91, 98–99, 124, 135–37; genitalia of, 38; as minority in France, 3, 6, 13, 17, 54; role of in shaping discussions of race and gender, 4, 15, 67–68, 87, 90, 101; role of in shaping French national identity, 3, 9, 11, 12, 15, 66, 79, 138; scholarship on, 11–12; as seductresses, 67, 98; sexual taboos and, 54, 75; white fantasies about, 3, 50, 87, 107. *See also* womanhood
Blainville, Henri de, 40
bohemian lifestyle: in Paris, 43; popularity of, 110. *See also* Baudelaire, Charles; Duval, Jeanne
Boilly, Louis Léopold, 51, 54; *Galeries du Palais-Royal*, 51, 53, 151n3
Bonaparte, Louis-Napoleon, 109
Bonaparte, Napoleon, 38, 59; anti-Napoleon publications, 58; Colnet's indignation at, 63; compassion toward, 64; crowned emperor, 55; followers of, 63–64; Napoleonic era, 60, 89; as symbol of colonial failure, 62–63, 78–79
Boufflers, Chevalier du, Stanislas Jean, 22–23, 28, 29, 85
Boulle, Pierre H., 26
Bourbon Dynasty, 10, 55
Brady, Heather, 88

Calvé, Emma, 48, 49
Carter, A. E., 129–30
Carter, Angela, 108
celebrity culture, 17, 58
Cesars, Hendrick, 30, 34, 146n28, 147n33
Christophe, Marc-A., 107, 120
Cohen, William, 5, 55, 148n39
Colnet du Ravel, Charles-Joseph Auguste: as exile, 58; on French masculinity, 59, 61, 62, 64; on Napoléon Bonaparte, 62–64; as royalist, 58, 63; as satirist, 58, 91; ventriloquism of Sarah Baartmann in writing, 58, 59, 60–64, 65–67, 68, 91, 93, 108–9. *See also* racial ventriloquism; white Frenchmen
colonial fantasies: Baartmann as subject of cultural and racial, 56; about black women, 50, 107, 135, 137; Duval as subject of cultural and racial, 124; about France's black colonies, 3, 57; about France's regaining of Saint-Domingue, 84; French racial discourses and, 87, 103; Orientalist, 24
colonialism, 3; anxieties about, 7, 15, 49, 68, 102, 108, 109, 132, 137, 142n23; and cosmopolitanism, 3; failure of, and black female bodies, 54; identity construction and, 4; and imperial domination, 36; inseparability of colony and metropole, 142n16; and mimicry, 102; racial hierarchies as justification for, 36, 41, 56; resistance to, 49; slavery and plantation society under, 10, 55; and tropes of savagery, 15. *See also* France; Frenchness; Haiti: French loss of; Haitian Revolution

colonial refugees, 54, 88, 138; from Haiti, 6, 67, 98. *See also* colonialism; exile; France; Paris; Saint-Domingue
consumer culture, 17, 49. *See also* Baartmann, Sarah; blackface; blackness; Ourika
Cordier, Charles-Henri-Joseph, 19–20, 144n3; *Vénus africaine*, 19, 20
cosmopolitanism, 1–3
Courbet, Gustave, 43; *L'Atelier du peintre*, 47, 106, 117, 118, 140, 150n71
Crais, Clifton C., 74, 146n26, 147n29, 147n33, 147n35, 148n39
Crofts, Marylee S., 91, 155n33
Cuvier, Georges Léopold, 16, 71; and Baartmann's cadaver, 38–40; manipulation of data about Baartmann, 40–42. *See also* racial science (scientific racism)

Darnton, Robert, 13
Daumier, Honoré, 43, 45
David, Jacques-Louis, 7, 142n17
Davis, Lennard J., 64
De Groot, Joanna, 37, 148n45
Delaplanche, Eugène, *L'Afrique*, 2
De Raedt, Thérèse, 24
de Tott, Sophie, 24; *Portrait d'Ourika*, 24, 25, 145n17
Du Camp, Maxime, 43
Dunlop, Alexander, 30, 33, 34, 147n29, 148n39
Duras, Claire de Durfort, Duchesse de: 14, 21, 23, 24, 96, 97, 108, 154n11, 155n24, 155n33; colonial ties of, 101; and exile, 88, 91; *Ourika*, 14, 81, 84, 85–92, 93, 154n19, 155n28; *Ourika*, contemporary responses to, 90–91
Duval, Jeanne, 14, 16–17, 21, 48, 50, 84, 138, 139, 140, 149n55, 149n56, 150n59, 150n64, 150n68; acting career of, 44–45, 131, 139, 150n60; in Baudelaire's letters, 43, 45, 46, 107–8, 110–12; birth of, 42; bohemian lifestyle of, 48, 110, 139; commodification of, 140; as common-law wife of Baudelaire, 16, 43, 45–47,

107; death of, 49, 151n73; erasure of from Courbet's painting, 106, 117, 150n71; family of, 42, 44, 46, 47; as fetish, 50; financial difficulties of, 45–47; Frenchness of, 107, 133, 138, 139; gender and, 110, 124, 129, 140; hospitalization of, 46, 150n68; as icon, 21; literary and visual depictions of, 14, 113–16, 117–20, 121, 150n71; and racial ventriloquism, 109; representations of, by Baudelaire's biographers, 108–9, 124–33; representations of, by Baudelaire's contemporaries, 108, 120–24; representations of, as prostitute, 126–27, 129, 130, 131, 139, 140; same-sex relationships, 157n2; as subject of racial and gendered attacks, 110; in works of black women artists and writers, 44. *See also* colonial fantasies; racial ventriloquism

Eichthal, Gustave d', 9
Eliel, Carol S., 51, 54, 151n3
empire vs. cosmopolitanism, 3
England: abolitionism in, 33–34; as major European power, 1; "Ourika Mania" in, 83; racism in, 49
exile: anti-Napoleon sentiments and, 63; aristocratic, 89; failure to assimilate and, 139

Fallaize, Elizabeth, 117
Fausto-Sterling, Anne, 40–41
female sexuality, iconography of, 36, 144n36
Fields, Jill, 74
Flaubert, Gustave, 105, 107
Fleming, John, 9
France: abolitionism in, 7, 19, 33, 55, 58, 88, 109; African colonies, 108, 110; ancien régime, 12, 55, 66, 109, 138; black colonies, 55, 67, 137; black population numbers in, 157n55; Caribbean colonies, 3, 9, 107; citizenship and nationhood questions, 4, 5, 10, 13, 55–56, 110, 138–39, 142n25; as colonial empire, 4, 5–6, 10, 16, 49, 110; colonialism, legitimization of, 41; colonial rhetoric, 91; divorce in, 152n29; fears of

INDEX 179

France (*continued*)
    racial inundation and contamination, 3, 141n4; imperial stature of, 6, 49, 54, 55–56, 63, 78, 79, 83; July Monarchy (1830–48), 16, 109; Louisiana, U.S. purchase of, 5; postcolonial era, 11; race, constructions of, 36, 101; racial mixing, anxieties about, 3; and refugees from Haiti, 6, 54, 56, 57, 67, 74, 91, 98, 138; representations of foreigners in, 77; Restoration (1814–30), 9, 55, 89, 90, 138; Revolution of 1830, 83, 110; Second Empire (1852–70), 5, 16, 109; and slave trade, 1–4, 9–10, 16, 17, 55, 58, 83–84, 100, 132, 139–40; West Indian colonies, 97; white homogeneity, perceived threats to, 6. *See also* colonialism; Haiti: French loss of; Haitian Revolution; Paris
Frenchness, 11, 21, 97, 140; authentic, 102; black bodies and, 13, 70; changing definitions of, 7, 9, 13, 15, 108, 139; colonialism and, 6, 7; and depictions of black women, 3, 7, 13, 57, 133; foreign elements and, 75; masculinity and, 59; and miscegenation, 102, 154n18; mythologizing of, 125; racialized tropes of, 66; rooted in brotherhood, 10; rooted in nobility, 10; as whiteness, 87, 101, 139
French Revolution, 4, 10, 13, 17, 87, 89, 138
Fuentes, Marisa J., 12

Gautier, Théophile, 43
Gay, Delphine, 96–97
Gazette de France, 58, 65
gender, 14, 55; changing attitudes toward, 138; codes of behavior related to, 67; cultural production of, 10; discursive, 9; and fears about emotional inauthenticity, 44; French constructions of, 4, 6, 12; in French society, tensions related to, 11, 102; intersections with race, 15, 36, 143n28; misogyny and, 64; and portrayals of black female bodies, 4; shifting categories of, 66, 96; transgression of proper roles, 68, 74, 79; ventriloquism and, 17, 91
Gilman, Sander L., 21, 36, 38, 144n4

Gilroy, Paul, 10, 144n24
Glyn, Anthony, 130–31

Haiti: French loss of, 5–6, 9, 10, 89, 97, 138; independence, 84; white settlers in, 88. *See also* Saint-Domingue
Haitian Revolution, 4–7, 13, 71, 87, 88, 89, 90; compensation of French colonials for loss of property, 84; demographic consequences of, 6; French attitudes toward, 4, 11, 15, 137; racial ramifications of, 55. *See also* Saint-Domingue
Harms, Robert W., 100
Hemmings, Frederick William John, 130, 149n56
Hesse, Carla, 10–11
Heuer, Jennifer, 143n28
Hoffmann, Léon-François, 98
Honour, Hugh, 9
"Hottentot Africans," 36–37, 149n47
Howland, John, 59
Hunt, Lynn, 10

Jenson, Deborah, 89
Journal de l'empire, 58
Journal de Paris, 58, 62, 95
Journal des dames et des modes, 68
Journal des débats politiques et littéraires, 84
Journal du commerce, 100

Kirby, Percival, 30, 146n36, 147n29
Kumar, Krishan, 6

La Tour du Pin, Marquise de Henriette Lucie Dillon, 24, 26
Little, Roger, 22, 23–24, 145n16
London Literary Gazette, 81, 95
Lowe, Kate, 23

Macaulay, Zachary, 33, 147n29, 147n31, 147n35
Manet, Édouard, 120, 125; *La Maîtresse de Baudelaire allongée*, 120, 121, 158n17; *Olympia*, 125, 159n27
Marie Antoinette, 23, 151n17
Martinet, Aaron, 72; *Les Curieux en extase;*

ou, *Les Cordons des souliers*, 73; *Le Prétexte*, 75, 76

Martinique, 85, 88; plantocracy in, 90; slave insurrection of 1822, 84; social and economic conditions of slavery in, 9; sugar and coffee plantations on, 3

Mathews, Charles, 32–33

Mathews, Mrs. Charles [Anne], 32–33

McClintock, Anne, 49, 79

McCloy, Shelby T., 23

melancholy: Baartmann's, 69; French, 63; Ourika's, 87

Memmi, Albert, 81

Miller, Christopher L., 88

Mills, Charles W., 137

miscegenation: desire for, 66–68; fear of, 75, 79, 98; interracial marriage and, 102; supposed sexual power of black women and, 98

Montesquieu, 58–59

Morrison, Toni, 105

Mosse, George, 37

Musée de l'homme, xiii–xv. *See also* Baartmann, Sarah

Nadar (Gaspard-Félix Tournachon): Duval as mistress of, 43; on Duval's sexuality, 129; recollections of Duval, 48, 123, 150n59; sees Duval performing as an actress, 44

Napoleon I. *See* Bonaparte, Napoleon

Napoleon III. *See* Bonaparte, Louis-Napoleon

Napoleonic Code, 10

Napoleonic Wars, 6

O'Connell, David, 88, 155n24

Ourika: as aristocratic woman, 139; baptism of, 23; birthplace of, 22; burial of, 145n22; Café Ourika, 99–101, 157n59; commodification of, 140; death of, 26, 28; emancipation, 26; and exile, 96; fads inspired by, 15, 81, 83; fashion inspired by, 92–93, 95; as fetish, 50; fragmentary information about, 49; Frenchness of, 88, 99, 101, 102, 138, 139; gender and, 90, 101, 140; given as a gift, 22, 24, 28; as historical personage, 14, 15, 16; hypervisuality of, 108; as icon, 21; literary depictions of, 14, 15, 85–90, 91, 96–99, 145n17, 153n3, 154n4, 154n11, 154n19, 155n28, 155n29, 156n39, 156n48; location of body, 145n22; and racial ventriloquism, 109; sexualized representations of, 24; signature of, 27; as subject of stage productions, 81, 84, 93–96; visual depictions of, 15, 24, 25, 28, 29, 30, 82. *See also* racial ventriloquism

"Ourika Mania," 14, 15, 81–84, 92, 101, 102, 103, 156n38, 156n45. *See also* melancholy

Paris, 45; actresses in, 95; colonial refugees in, 6; as cosmopolitan center, 1; historical changes in society of, 109, 110; influence of foreigners on city natives, 78; Josephine Baker as sensation in, 135; Museum of Natural History in, 19, 20; nonwhite population of, 3; Ourika baptized in, 23; "Ourika Mania" in, 81, 83, 93, 99; prostitution in, 51, 53, 54; Rétif de la Bretonne's writings about, 51; salons in, 85, 90; social circles in, 24, 30; Théâtre du Panthéon in, 44, 45

Peabody, Sue, 3–4, 154n11, 157n55

Pichois, Claude, 45, 124, 131, 149n55, 150n59, 150n60

Pons, Gaspard de, 96–99

Popkin, Jeremy, 5

Porché, François, 125–27

Prarond, Ernest, 43, 122

Prasad, Pratima, 88, 154n19

prostitution, 42, 140; depictions in art, 51, 54; depictions of black women and, 54; theatre acting associated with, 44, 131, 139

race: and French identity, 9, 88, 138, 139; in historical studies, 151n6; intersections with gender, 9, 15, 36, 148n40; racial essentialism, 154n16; racial hierarchies, as justification for colonialism, 36; racial hierarchies, permeability of, 75; scientific discussions of, 36, 37, 148n45; transgression of proper roles, 138

racial drag, 83, 91
racial mimicry, 83, 101–2
racial science (scientific racism), 36–37, 38, 49. *See also* Cuvier, Georges Léopold
racial ventriloquism, 17, 58, 91, 109, 124, 138, 140
Racine, Jean, 51
Rétif de la Bretonne, N. E., 51, 151n2
Reynold, Gonzague de, 43, 125
Richon, Emmanuel, 124, 151n73

Sabran, Delphine de, 22
Said, Edward, 13
Saint-Domingue, 84, 85; as crown jewel of France's colonial empire, 4–5; Duras's relation to, 88, 89, 97; Duval's relation to, 42; French loss of, 6–7, 66, 138; racial anxieties in, 137; refugees from, 91, 98; revolution in, 87, 90; sugar and coffee plantations in, 3. *See also* Haiti; Haitian Revolution
Schiebinger, Londa, 1
Scully, Pamela, 74, 146n26, 147n29, 147n33, 147n35, 148n39. *See also* Crais, Clifton C.
Senegal, 15, 22–24, 85, 110
Sepinwall, Alyssa Goldstein, 5, 154n16
Sharpley-Whiting, T. Deanan, 36, 40, 74, 97, 144n4
slavery: colonial, 55; and cultural attitudes toward black women, 9, 10, 109; in France, 19, 55, 109, 138, 139; literary depictions of, 86, 89, 94–95, 98, 154n19; white, 70
slave trade, European participation in, 1, 34. *See also* France
Smalls, James, 6, 144n3
Starkie, Enid, 127–28, 129
Stoler, Ann, 110, 132

Théaulon de Lambert, Marie-Emmanuel-Guillaume-Marguerite, 64
Tillotson, Victoria P., 108
Toubin, Charles, 43, 120
Tournachon, Gaspard-Félix (Nadar): Duval as mistress of, 43; on Duval's sexuality, 129; recollections of Duval, 48, 123,
150n59; sees Duval performing as an actress, 44
Turnell, Martin, 128

Vieillard, Pierre-Ange, 96, 98

white Frenchmen: associated with civilization, 68; attitudes toward Baartmann, 38, 54, 74, 78; attitudes toward Duval, 110, 117, 122, 124–25; attitudes toward Ourika, 84, 92, 101, 102; attitudes toward revolution in Saint-Domingue, 5; bad behavior of, 59, 93; and the colonial self, 6; and definitions of Frenchness, 15; Duval's father and grandfather as, 42; and fantasies about France's black colonies, 3; and fashion, 14, 93; and loss of the colonies, 57; and minstrelsy, 91; perception of black women, 17, 21, 50, 65–66, 75, 83, 91, 108; and portrayals of black female bodies, 4, 54, 122; and racial ventriloquism, 58; relationships with nonwhite women, 18; and scientific dominance over white and black women, 41; sex with black women, 99; shopping habits of, 78
white Frenchwomen: associated with beauty, 68; attitudes toward Baartmann, 54, 74; attitudes toward Duval, 110, 117, 122; attitudes toward Ourika, 84, 92, 101, 102; attitudes toward revolution in Saint-Domingue, 5; bad behavior of, 59, 72, 78; bodies of, 15, 41; calls for moral regulation of, 64; and the colonial self, 6; compared to Hottentot women, 60; and definitions of Frenchness, 15; and fantasies about France's black colonies, 3; and fashion, 14; and minstrelsy, 91, 95, 103; and national identity, 79; perceptions of black women, 17, 21, 50, 83, 91, 108; and portrayals of black female bodies, 4, 54, 122; representations of as manipulative, 66; shopping habits of, 78
white imagination, 71, 72, 87, 99, 103, 139. *See also* blackness
whiteness: aristocracy and, 23, 86; associated

with beauty, 69, 75; and authenticity, 132; and black womanhood, 125; and French identity, 67, 87, 109–10, 138; and the male gaze, 137; and maleness, 71, 138; as opposite of blackness, 87, 107; and racial homogeneity, 6; reinforcement of tropes about, 11; and segregation, 94–95; social constructions of, 139; as superior to blackness, 36, 41, 79, 90, 98. *See also* colonial fantasies; Frenchness

Wilson, Elizabeth, 44

womanhood: black, 83, 87, 96, 107, 109, 125; elevation of European, 54; French, 97, 99; white, 96, 98, 99. *See also* black women; white Frenchwomen; whiteness

Woolf, Virginia, 19

RACE IN THE ATLANTIC WORLD, 1700–1900

*The Hanging of Angélique: The Untold Story of
Canadian Slavery and the Burning of Old Montréal*
BY AFUA COOPER

*Christian Ritual and the Creation of
British Slave Societies, 1650–1780*
BY NICHOLAS M. BEASLEY

*African American Life in the Georgia Lowcountry:
The Atlantic World and the Gullah Geechee*
EDITED BY PHILIP MORGAN

*The Horrible Gift of Freedom: Atlantic Slavery
and the Representation of Emancipation*
BY MARCUS WOOD

*The Life and Letters of Philip Quaque,
the First African Anglican Missionary*
EDITED BY VINCENT CARRETTA AND TY M. REESE

*In Search of Brightest Africa: Reimagining the
Dark Continent in American Culture, 1884–1936*
BY JEANNETTE EILEEN JONES

*Contentious Liberties: American Abolitionists in
Post-emancipation Jamaica, 1834–1866*
BY GALE L. KENNY

*We Are the Revolutionists: German-Speaking
Immigrants and American Abolitionists after 1848*
BY MISCHA HONECK

The American Dreams of John B. Prentis, Slave Trader
BY KARI J. WINTER

*Missing Links: The African and American
Worlds of R. L. Garner, Primate Collector*
BY JEREMY RICH

*Almost Free: A Story about Family and Race
in Antebellum Virginia*
BY EVA SHEPPARD WOLF

*To Live an Antislavery Life: Personal Politics
and the Antebellum Black Middle Class*
BY ERICA L. BALL

*Flush Times and Fever Dreams: A Story of
Capitalism and Slavery in the Age of Jackson*
BY JOSHUA D. ROTHMAN

*Diplomacy in Black and White: John Adams,
Toussaint Louverture, and Their Atlantic World Alliance*
BY RONALD ANGELO JOHNSON

*Enterprising Women: Gender, Race, and Power
in the Revolutionary Atlantic*
BY KIT CANDLIN AND CASSANDRA PYBUS

*Eighty-Eight Years: The Long Death of Slavery
in the United States, 1777–1865*
BY PATRICK RAEL

*Finding Charity's Folk:
Enslaved and Free Black Women in Maryland*
BY JESSICA MILLWARD

*The Mulatta Concubine: Terror, Intimacy,
Freedom, and Desire in the Black Transatlantic*
BY LISA ZE WINTERS

*The Politics of Black Citizenship: Free African Americans
in the Mid-Atlantic Borderland, 1817–1863*
BY ANDREW K. DIEMER

*Punishing the Black Body: Marking Social and
Racial Structures in Barbados and Jamaica*
BY DAWN P. HARRIS

Race and Nation in the Age of Emancipations
EDITED BY WHITNEY NELL STEWART AND
JOHN GARRISON MARKS

*Vénus Noire: Black Women and Colonial Fantasies
in Nineteenth-Century France*
BY ROBIN MITCHELL

*City of Refuge: Slavery and Petit Marronage
in the Great Dismal Swamp, 1763–1856*
BY MARCUS P. NEVIUS

www.ingramcontent.com/pod-product-compliance
Lightning Source LLC
Chambersburg PA
CBHW011720220426
43664CB00023B/2900